Law, Informal Rules and Economic Performance

To Susan, with love and gratitude

Law, Informal Rules and Economic Performance

The Case for Common Law

Svetozar Pejovich

Professor Emeritus, Texas A&M University, USA, Honorary Doctorate, University of Belgrade, Serbia, and Professor of Law and Economics, University of Donja Gorica, Montenegro

with contributions from

Enrico Colombatto

Professor of Economics, School of Economics, University of Turin, Italy

Edward Elgar
Cheltenham, UK • Northampton, MA, USA

Published by
Edward Elgar Publishing Limited
Glensanda House
Montpellier Parade
Cheltenham
Glos GL50 1UA
UK

Edward Elgar Publishing, Inc.
William Pratt House
9 Dewey Court
Northampton
Massachusetts 01060
USA

A catalogue record for this book
is available from the British Library

Library of Congress Control Number: 2008927693

ISBN 978 1 84542 873 0 (cased)

Typeset by Manton Typesetters, Louth, Lincolnshire, UK
Printed and bound in Great Britain by MPG Books Ltd, Bodmin, Cornwall

Contents

Tables

Foreword

Leonard P. Liggio*

Svetozar Pejovich has been a leading scholar of the economics of property rights. His writings and his conference participations in Europe and America have contributed to the profession's understanding of important concepts in law and economics.

In *Law, Informal Rules and Economic Performance*, Pejovich presents us with an overview of the issues on which he has worked for many years. In his famous comment, Sir Henry Maine stated that modern civilization represented the movement from status to contract. Behind that crucial movement was the emergence of the rule of law. It is the role of the rule of law in the transition to modern civilization which is described by Pejovich.

The rule of law makes possible the enforcement of property rights; and property rights make possible man's progressive adoption of new technology to new challenges. Pejovich examines the different consequences of the two major Western legal systems. The Anglo-American legal tradition of common law emphasizes the continuity of legal principles applied to different or new circumstances. The process of seeking answers for the future from the decisions of the past gives the common law the space for growth.

The Continental legal system founded on the civil code seeks a different route to meet challenges. Professor Enrico Colombatto of the University of Turin in Italy has contributed sections on the Italian and Swiss constitutions as well as discussing the book with the author. Pejovich indicated the role of the evolution of the legal process in the example of the medieval Law Merchant. He draws on the important historical contributions of Harold Berman and Deepak Lal regarding the Western legal tradition.

Pejovich presents the modern economic analysis pioneered by John Locke, Bernard Mandeville, David Hume and Adam Smith. He expands this by the introduction of issues, such as transaction costs, by contemporary social scientists: Armen Alchian, Ronald Coase, Harold Demsetz, Henry Manne, Douglass North and Oliver Williamson.

---

* Law School, George Mason University

The role of the entrepreneur deservedly gains the attention of Pejovich, who draws on the economic schools of Market Process and of Public Choice to develop the importance of entrepreneurship in economics.

The reader is presented with clear writing and full explanations. Pejovich has made a welcomed contribution to the economics literature.

L.P.L.

Preface and acknowledgments

This book is about capitalism and its economic performance. Capitalism is the only system in recorded history that has been successful in pulling the average person above the subsistence level and sustaining a steady, if cyclical, rate of economic development. Yet, from the very beginning, capitalism has had numerous critics.

The twentieth century witnessed the rise and failure of two major anti-capitalist movements: National Socialism and Marxism–Leninism. These movements shared many basic premises of socialist doctrine. They advocated a command economy, despised private property rights, and pursued the objectives of the ruling elite at the expense of the right of individuals to pursue their own ends. The demise of command economies in the late 1980s did not discourage the critics of capitalism. Without missing a beat, they aligned themselves with the welfare state and social democracies. As we enter the twenty-first century, environmentalism, multiculturalism, welfarism and EU bureaucracy have become the homes for the critics of capitalism.

In addition to the systems that have been tried to replace capitalism, many critics find capitalism, *as it exists*, inferior to blackboard models that *have never existed*. Karl Brunner summarized the contribution of this group of critics as follows: 'The sacrifice of cognition is particularly easy to detect in objections to the market system introduced by discrepancies between one's desires, glorified as social values, and the results of market processes. However, our ability to visualize 'better' states more closely reflecting our preferences yields no evidence that this state can be realized.'

Notwithstanding the multitude of its critics, capitalism has passed the most important test: the test of time. Capitalism has not only outlived its critics but is spreading, albeit unevenly, throughout the world; from China to Chile, the standard of living is rising in countries that have adopted or are adopting its basic institutions.

The purpose of this book is not to advocate capitalism on philosophical or ideological grounds or to claim that its system of values is superior to those of other systems. In free societies, those decisions should be made by individuals in accordance with their values and beliefs. My key purpose is to explain why the system has done so well. Toward that end, the analysis follows two interrelated paths. The first is analysis of the incentive effects of the formal and informal institutions of capitalism on the economic behavior of individuals; or, to phrase this another way, analysis of the effects of capitalist rules on the game itself. The second is the examination of adjustments in the rules over time. The success of capitalism since its birth some time in the sixteenth century suggests that the system has been able to create new institutions continuously in response to changes in technology. That is, the system has been effective in adjusting the rules to the changing requirements of the game. Hence, an important purpose of this book is to explore how and why the incentive effects of the basic institutions of capitalism have been successful in responding to changes in the economic conditions of life.

In pursuing those objectives, I identify two major types of capitalism – Anglo-American capitalism and Continental capitalism – and the two legal systems upon which the two types depend, so as to explain how and why different versions of capitalism have led to different socioeconomic results.

Part I discusses some basic economic concepts, the importance of transaction costs, the role of institutions and, very importantly, the meaning of economic efficiency based on the Austrian and Public Choice schools (Chapters 1–2). The definition of economic efficiency is consistently used throughout the book. Readers familiar with mainstream neoclassical economics need not agree with this definition of efficiency; it suffices to understand the context in which the term *economic efficiency* is used.

After brief discussion of the birth of capitalism and its dependence on the rule of law, Part II is an analysis of the incentive effects of four basic institutions of capitalism embodied in the rule of law (Chapters 3–9). Chapter 8 relates the incentive effects of the institutions of capitalism to economic performance.

In Part III I propose and develop a theory of efficiency-friendly institutional changes that are consistent with both the culture of capitalism and sustainable economic development (Chapters 10–15). This theory of efficiency-friendly institutional changes rests on three major factors: the rule of law, the carriers of change, and the interaction between formal and informal institutions. By arguing that the rule of law provides incentives for the carriers of change to narrow the gap between the culture of capitalism and the prevailing culture in the community, the proposed theory introduces culture into the model.

While I am fully responsible for the analysis, ideas and concepts expressed, I owe thanks to a number of friends and colleagues. My greatest gratitude goes to Enrico Colombatto, Professor of Economics at the University of Turin, with whom I discussed at great length many of the ideas put forward in these pages, especially in Part II. In addition, Professor Colombatto authored the sections on the Italian and Swiss constitutions in Chapter 6.

Others who provided important suggestions and criticism are Ljubo Madzar, professor at Braca Karic University in Belgrade; John Moore, president-emeritus of Grove City College; William Murchison, a syndicated columnist and professor of journalism at Baylor University; and Dallas attorney Gary Short. Eric Weede of the University of Colon has influenced my views on the contribution of Max Weber to the rise of capitalism.

Gerald O'Driscoll's Liberty Find conference on 'Law, Liberty and Trading States' (Santa Fe, New Mexico on 9–12 March 2006), helped me to appreciate the development of private laws in the Middle Ages as well as the supremacy of common law over civil law. Discussions with colleagues and students at the University of Freiburg and Max Planck Institute in Jena sharpened my understanding of the relationship between formal institutions and culture. I am grateful to the Liberty Fund for the opportunity to attend several conferences in Europe and the United States to discuss the role of law and culture in economic development.

As always, Sally Antrobus of Seabrook, Texas, provided excellent editorial assistance.

PART I

Basic economic concepts

1. The game and the rules of the game

Economic life involves two levels of social activity: the development and maintenance of institutions, or the rules of the game; and exchange within the prevailing institutional framework, or the game itself. This chapter discusses some basic and well known principles of economic life at both levels of social activity. While discussion is elementary, it is also necessary for better understanding of the rest of this book.

THE GAME: SOME FUNDAMENTAL ECONOMIC CONCEPTS

No matter how affluent or poor we are as individuals or as a nation, what we want exceeds what is available. Ask yourself if there is something that you would like to have but have not been able to afford. You can ask others. They will probably say they have many desires that are yet to be satisfied. A high school teacher might believe that wealthy corporate CEOs have satisfied all their wants. Before speaking, however, the teacher should ask the CEOs if they really have everything *they* want. On the issues of tastes, wants, desires and feelings, we can only speak for ourselves. And speaking for ourselves, we know that we have unsatisfied wants. The fiasco in the Garden of Eden, the mercilessness of nature, too many people, and many other causes have been blamed for giving us fewer goods than we believe we should have. Whatever or whoever might be causally responsible for this sad but indisputable fact of life, the gap between what we want and what is available does exist.

The desire for more satisfaction is a predictable consequence of the gap between what we have and what is available. In fact, the desire for more satisfaction has been the major observable trait of human behavior throughout recorded history. Armen Alchian argued that the desire for more satisfaction is a survival trait, which has enabled us to survive competition from other forms of life. The US Constitution refers to the desire for more satisfaction as the pursuit of happiness. Neoclassical economists have converted it into the maximization paradigm. Most economists use the classical term 'self-interest'. In this light, pursuing self-interest acquires the status of a legitimate goal for all individuals, important enough to justify constitutional protection.

The desire for more satisfaction or the pursuit of self-interest is not to be confused with sometimes pejorative reference to selfishness. Self-interest means that, whenever a person faces a choice between two or more sources of satisfaction, that person will choose the alternative expected to yield benefits in excess of the costs. Those who prefer Coke to Pepsi do not buy Pepsi; those who prefer BMW to Fiat, buy BMW; and those who enjoy mountains are not likely to vacation in seaside resorts.

Scarcity and Opportunity Costs

To say that what we want exceeds what is available means that we are all seeking more goods. It is not important whether the things we want are material or not. They may be physical objects (e.g., milk), non-physical things (e.g., friendship), activities (e.g., a church service), or doing things for others (helping handicapped individuals). The power of things to yield satisfaction is what really matters. Thus, a *good* is anything that yields satisfaction to someone. Meat is a good for me but it is not for my vegetarian friends, unless they change their preference. Individuals satisfy their wants by acquiring and/or consuming goods. For us to acquire and/or consume them, the goods have to be produced.

To choose what we prefer does not mean we always get more satisfaction. The term 'expected' means that our choices have future implications that, at best, can only be anticipated. A Coke may be flat, a BMW might turn out to be a lemon, and the Church might do things we do not like. The best we can do is to choose alternatives we prefer and keep our fingers crossed. The fact that most communities protect people who are either incapable (e.g., mentally deranged) or presumed to be incapable (e.g., children) of making choices for themselves is good evidence that the desire for more satisfaction is a survival behavior.

The fact that what we want exceeds what is available has given rise to the two most important economic concepts: *scarcity and opportunity costs*. Scarcity means that, to get a little more of any good, a little of some other good has to be given up. And that little bit of something else that has to be given up is called the opportunity cost. The opportunity cost is then the value of that which is being given up. Every time a person spends five dollars on pizza, that person gives up the satisfaction from another bundle of goods that five dollars could buy. A student deciding to study on a Saturday night gives up the satisfaction of going out on a date. No matter how affluent or poor we are as individuals, scarcity is with us.

Resources

To produce goods requires resources including time (e.g., the time required to develop a friendship has alternative uses). Things become resources only after someone discovers that they could be converted into useful goods and/or someone converts them into useful goods. For example, oil had been known to Indians in Texas or to Sarmatas along the northern shores of the Black Sea for a long time before it became a resource. That is, resources are created, not found. Once they are created, we seek more of them.

In response to the human search for more satisfaction, entrepreneurs continuously create new resources. The creation of new resources should then be expected to shrink the gap between what we want and what we have. Unfortunately, it has yet to happen. We observe no difference in the behavior of individuals in developed and underdeveloped countries. While the volume of wants they are able to satisfy is not the same, they all behave as if they had unsatisfied desires. It appears as if new wants are created at the same rate or at an even higher rate than the rate at which the existing wants are satisfied.

Louis XIV never had an opportunity to develop a desire to wear nylon shirts, while most of today's students do. President Wilson had to put up with Washington's heat while his successors 'couldn't live' in the city without air conditioners. Henry Ford never owned a computer, but most children today do not think that having a computer is a big deal. The author of this book has developed a completely new desire during his recent visit to Italy. He now wants a luxury villa in the Italian Alps.

Unless the behavior of people in the future turns out to be different from human behavior over the last several thousand years, we can conclude that human wants are limitless. A critical feature of resources is that they have alternative uses. A person can be either barber or salesperson but cannot be both. The land used to build a football stadium could have been used to build private residences. A student can choose a more active social life or spend more hours studying for a test in economics. Each time we use a resource to produce goods that satisfy a want, we are choosing not to use that resource to satisfy other wants. And that point applies not only to individuals but to the community as well. The community could have cleaner air and cleaner water at a cost of reducing the supply of homes, cars, planes and other goods we also value. The next time a politician tells you that we need more schools, ask what it is that we should do without.

Who gets what and *who does what* are thus the two fundamental survival issues that all societies have had to deal with since the beginning of history. Indeed, they have done so in many different ways. Among the most often observed methods people have historically relied upon to resolve the issues of who gets what and who does what are price competition, violence and bribery; first-come, first-served (queuing) and personal connections; physical attributes such as female beauty; and government planning. All these methods favor some people (e.g., violence favors stronger men) and discriminate against others (e.g., first-come, first-served discriminates against people too weak or busy to stand in lines). This means we cannot escape discrimination in choosing who gets what and who does what (the act of choice is the act of discrimination); however, we can choose the method by which we discriminate. Historically, the most productive method for resolving those two issues has been price competition leading to free exchange or trade.

Exchange or Trade

Production and exchange are two sides of the same coin. Production means using resources to produce goods. It means that resources yield satisfaction to those who use them to produce goods. To obtain command over resources, producers have to enter into agreements with those who control resources. Thus, for reasons of convenience, this book treats production as exchange.

Exchange or trade is a means by which individuals seek more satisfaction for themselves. The method of payment by one of the parties could be money or other goods; in exchange for using a colleague's office I might proof-read his book. People enter into exchange because they expect that their benefits from acquiring a good will exceed their costs.

The benefit from exchange is the increment in satisfaction a person derives from acquiring a good. The value of any good to a person depends on the expected flow of benefits from that good. The cost of exchange is the satisfaction a person has to give up. When someone spends $100 on books, the real cost of those books is the satisfaction given up by not choosing to spend $100 on another bundle of goods. By enjoying the satisfaction of an active social life, a student gives up the satisfaction of a higher grade. The term 'expects' says that, in a world of uncertainty and incomplete information, the future consequences of our current decisions cannot be fully predicted. A marriage may fall apart; a chocolate bar may make you sick.

New knowledge about exchange opportunities affects the price by modifying our perception of the expected flow of benefits from that good. Once I discover that I love Czech beer, Schlitz would have to lower its price to keep my business. And changes in the bundle of rights in a good that is being exchanged affect the price we are willing to pay for that good. The value of a car to me is less if I have no right to resell it; I pay more to join a country club if my teenage kids are allowed to play golf there; and I value my house more if I have a right to exclude gasoline stations from the neighborhood.

In a world of uncertainty and incomplete information (hereafter referred to as 'the world of bounded rationality'), individuals have different perceptions of the set of available exchange opportunities. Moreover, no two people are alike in terms of their talents, personality traits, looks, aspirations and tastes. Thus, each individual has particular preferences. Those preferences are subjective and, therefore, not known to others. Some choose to negotiate exchanges that others find unattractive. Eventually, individuals reveal their preferences via the process of making an exchange.

When people spend $1000 on a suit, or $30 on beer, or give $100 at church, they inform others that the satisfaction they expect – and we emphasize the term 'expect' – to get from that suit, beer or contribution to the church exceeds the satisfaction from another bundle of goods worth $1000, $30 or $100. Of course, exchange is not limited to trading goods for money. A student going to a bar on the evening before an important exam tells us, in effect, that the satisfaction of spending the evening drinking with friends exceeds that of a higher grade, which several additional hours of study could make possible.

To say that exchange makes us better off does not mean we carry with us small computers to calculate the increments of satisfaction we expect to derive from each and every exchange. Sometimes we agonize over a decision (e.g., choosing a home), sometimes we act on impulse (e.g., buying a pizza while dieting) and sometimes we act out of habit (e.g., going to the same restaurant). However, human behavior is consistent in one respect. By changing the bundle of other things a person has to give up in exchange for one unit of any good, say a juicy Texas steak, we can influence the frequency with which that person eats steaks.

The bundle of other things that anyone is willing to give up in exchange for one unit of a good depends on preference and income. In the case of exchanges that have long-run consequences, the attitudes individuals have toward risk and uncertainty also affect the terms of exchange. Economists are not interested in why human preferences are what they are. Economists are concerned with the issue of how and why human preferences translate into observed behavior. To that end, let us start with two observations.

First, the law of diminishing marginal utility directly influences the translation of each person's preferences into observed behavior. A person's total consumption of beer per unit of time (e.g., an evening) depends on the rate at which the satisfaction of drinking successive bottles of beer falls relative to the satisfaction from other goods that have to be sacrificed in exchange for each bottle of beer. And a person who drinks one glass of calvados every night would discover that an increase in the price of calvados would mean having to forgo the satisfaction from a larger bundle of other goods. The drinker has incentives to reduce the consumption of calvados.

Second, as individuals go through the process of choosing among subjectively evaluated alternatives, they acquire new knowledge about the satisfaction they derive from various goods, and they also develop new wants. And the diffusion of this knowledge continuously modifies individuals' preferences from within the system and creates new exchange opportunities (i.e., innovation). After encountering Tex-Mex cooking, an Italian in Texas is less likely to go looking for Italian food.

The role of income in the process of making choices is important but easy to exaggerate. Income is primarily a constraint that defines one's set of choices. In a market economy the size of our incomes depends on what our services are worth to others. And, given our incomes, we make choices in accordance with our preferences. Even when equipped with $100 per day to spend, a person may choose to forgo a second beer when the price of beer increases from one to two dollars. The satisfaction that person derives from other goods (e.g., ice cream) that two dollars could buy is the major factor affecting the choice. On the other hand, someone with only $50 per day to spend and a serious love of beer may continue to buy beer at a higher price.

To say that the satisfaction one person receives from purchasing a good from another is subjective means that a third person could not make an informed decision for the first one. It is entirely possible for a third person to have better information about the consequences of the exchange that the first two are contemplating. However, there is no way for the third person to know better the subjective satisfaction that the others expect to derive from that exchange. We observe that a number of people continue to smoke even though the government has mandated that each pack of cigarettes must carry a specific health warning. The message is quite simple. The satisfaction smokers get from tobacco exceeds their estimate of the risk of contracting lung cancer; that is, they choose to use a high discount rate in evaluating the future consequences of their current decision to smoke. The urge some people have to protect others from making a 'wrong choice' takes away from individuals the right to make their own choice, including the choice of risk. Consequently, the people whom they try to 'help to stay well' end up being worse off.

Mandating choices fails to produce good economic results because of a huge gap between the preferences of those making allocative decisions (even when they have better information) and those for whom those decisions are made. Mandated choices are frequently justified by reference to general welfare or the public interest. The problem with those terms is that they assume that the social welfare function exists, that public decision makers know it, and that they are unselfishly going to implement it. None of these three assumptions is derivable from scientific knowledge.

Providing or selling information about the expected future consequences of one's choice and leaving people free to choose the risk they are willing to bear makes more sense than imposing someone else's subjective preference upon them. My doctor knows better the effects of pizza on my health but only I know how much risk I am willing to take in order to satisfy my desire for pizza. The doctor is paid to give information and I am free to act upon it.

The difference between mandated welfare and the freedom to choose one's contributions is the difference between collectivism and individual liberty. That is so because unilateral exchange (e.g., charitable giving) is a source of satisfaction. When I donate $1000 to an orphanage, the satisfaction I expect to derive from this tax deductible (unilateral) exchange is more valuable than whatever satisfaction I could get from another bundle that $1000 could buy.

The United States tax system gives people incentives to be charitable via liberal tax deductions on their spending. Predictably, Americans gave nearly $300 billion to charitable causes in 2006, setting a new record. About 65 percent of households with incomes less than $100000 gave to charity. The biggest chunk of the donations, $96.82 billion or 32.8 percent, went to religious organizations. The second largest slice, $40.98 billion or 13.9 percent, went to education, including gifts to colleges, universities and libraries. As a percentage of gross domestic products, the U.S. ranked first at 1.7 percent, the United Kingdom gave 0.73 percent, and a welfare state like France only 0.14 percent.[1]

An example with which most children are familiar is also the best evidence that we give money and other gifts to enhance *our* satisfaction. Suppose an Italian professor intends to give a computer to his high school daughter for Christmas. The computer costs 1000 euros. The daughter asks her father to give her 1000 euros in cash, instead. I could always choose to spend 1000 euros to buy a computer, she says. But, should I choose to spend 1000 euros on something else I like better than a computer, I would get more satisfaction at the same cost to you. Yet things do not work that way in most families. Parents do not want to maximize their kids' satisfaction; they want their kids to have what parents think should maximize their (children's) satisfaction.

Meaning of Economic Efficiency

In the world of bounded rationality, we perceive and evaluate exchange opportunities subjectively. Given our desire for more satisfaction, exchange is the most important method for improving our well-being. Voluntary choices we make in the pursuit of self-interest have an unintended consequence of moving goods from those who value them less to those who value them more. *The economic efficiency of the use of resources to produce goods and the allocation of goods among competing uses is then expressed in the process through which voluntary interactions are carried out, leading into the unknown.* Economic efficiency should not be judged by the attainment of a predetermined desirable outcome or by its quantitative dimensions. This definition of economic efficiency is used throughout the book.

THE RULES OF THE GAME OR INSTITUTIONS

In the pursuit of self-interest, individuals interact with one another. Some exchanges are simultaneous: I buy a book and give the seller $20. On the other hand, many exchanges involve decisions that have future value consequences. Examples are investing in stocks, buying on credit, getting married and paying tuition now in exchange for receiving educational services later on. Given uncertainty about the future, there is a built-in-bias in favor of decisions that are simultaneous or short-term, yet our personal wealth and economic development depend on decisions that have value consequences in the future.

The extent of exchange depends on removing the built-in bias in favor of decisions that are simultaneous. The removal of this bias is contingent on each person's ability to anticipate the behavior of others. And the predictability of other people's behavior presupposes the existence of a set of rules or institutions. Institutions are then the legal, administrative and customary arrangements for enhancing repeated human interactions. Institutions in themselves do not guarantee the predictability of behavior. In order for us to be able to predict human behavior, institutions must be credible (i.e., enforced) and stable (i.e., not subject to frequent change, so as to extend individuals' time horizon).

Rules that are loosely enforced raise the transaction costs of trade within the community and, even more so, with individuals in other communities. The rules also need to be stable. The more stable the rules are, the easier it is for individuals to enter into exchanges that have future value consequences. It is only in a stable institutional environment that individuals can take time to adjust to the rules, identify exchange opportunities those rules create, and choose the ones they prefer.

The prevailing institutions in any society consist of informal and formal rules. The ratio of formal to informal rules has increased with the transformation of medieval institutions into the modern ones.

Informal Institutions

Early in human history, individuals discovered that forming groups enhanced their survival chances in a hostile environment. To capture the benefits from forming groups, individuals had to learn how to interact with one another. It is safe to conjecture that many different groups tried different types of interactions. It is also safe to say that some forms of interactions failed to secure the survival of the groups that tried them, while other types of interactions had positive survival traits.

Then as now, the behaviors producing positive survival results would be repeated, marginally adjusted through time to changing circumstances, and transferred from one generation to another. Eventually they would become institutionalized into informal rules, not necessarily because members of the group understood them but because of their survival potential. By trial and error, different groups adopted different informal rules and developed their own path dependencies.

Informal rules, then, are traditions, customs, moral values, religious beliefs and all the other norms of behavior that have emerged spontaneously, survived the test of time and served to bind the generations. They are transmitted from one generation to another via oral interpretation of history, teaching, imitation and, of course, grandparents' stories. Informal rules are also called culture, the old ethos, the carriers of history and the hand of the past. Whatever one chooses to call them, informal rules are the repository of community values and are enforced by means of sanctions that include loss of reputation, ostracism by friends and neighbors, expulsion from the community and, less frequently, more severe forms of punishment. In this book I use the terms 'culture', 'customs' and 'tradition', and informal institutions interchangeably.

Adherence to informal rules by individual members of any community is hardly ever the same. The behavior of some individuals in the community is always below the accepted margin, while the behavior of some others is above it. Yet all communities have their mainstream informal rules of the game, which identify their prevailing cultures and are the results of selective evolution. Informal rules and their economic implications are discussed in Part III of this book.

Formal Institutions

Formal rules are constitutions, statutes, common laws and other governmental regulations. They define the political system (the hierarchical structure, decision-making powers, and individuals' rights); the economic system (property rights in scarce resources, contracts); and the protection system (judiciary, military, police). Governments enforce formal rules by means of sanctions such as fines, imprisonment and execution.

Bruno Leoni and Friedrich Hayek have generalized the origin of formal institutions in the West into the Continental and the Anglo-American traditions, which are more fully addressed in Chapter 3. The Continental tradition emphasizes formal rules that are enacted by legislators, while the Anglo-American tradition accentuates the spontaneous development of formal rules by common law courts. The economic consequences of these two traditions are discussed in Part II.

The major premise of this book is that changes in institutions, formal and informal, affect the economy, and that changes in the economy have predictable effects on the development and modification of institutions. Since capitalism has produced economic results that no other system has been able to duplicate, my analysis of the relationship between institutions and economic performance emphasizes the philosophical and legal foundations of capitalism, its institutions and their interactions with the economic forces at work. The positive line of reasoning throughout the book is simple and straightforward: institutions create their own behavioral incentives. Different incentives have different effects on the transaction costs of exchange. And different transaction costs have different effects on the extent of exchange and the flow of innovation.

This reasoning also raises a normative issue: is it possible, and if so how, to move the community toward capitalism via voluntary interactions among freely-choosing individuals and with only limited involvement of the state? It is an important question because the transition process in Central and Eastern Europe has demonstrated that the transaction costs of institutional changes imposed from the top down are significant. The best evidence is that many countries have socialists or other pro-collectivist parties back into power.

NOTES

1.   Vinner Tong (2007), *AP Business Report*, 25 June. See also Claire Gaudiani (2004), *The Greater Good*, Goldensville,Virginia: Holt Henry & Co.

2. Transaction costs

In a world of bounded rationality, the rules are costly to produce, monitor and enforce, and the game is costly to play. Thus transaction costs, as those costs are called, are the costs of all resources required for playing the game (e.g., discovering exchange opportunities, negotiating exchange, monitoring the fulfillment of contracts and enforcing the terms of exchange) and for developing, maintaining and protecting the rules of the game (e.g., judiciary, police, armed forces). The transaction costs have an effect on the extent of exchange in the community, the flow of innovation, and the maintenance of prevailing institutions.

Ronald Coase, a Nobel laureate, was perhaps the first economist to pay serious attention to the importance of transaction costs. He wrote (1988, p. 175): 'The reason why economists went wrong was that their theoretical system did not take into account a factor which is essential if one wishes to analyze the effect of a change in the law on the allocation of resources. This missing factor is the existence of transaction costs.' Academic research by scholars such as Armen Alchian, Harold Demsetz, Henry Manne, Doug North and Oliver Williamson supports Coase's analysis of the importance of transaction costs, as does empirical evidence. As shown in Chapters 11 and 12, the transition process in post-socialist Central and Eastern Europe provides the most compelling and recent evidence about the importance of transaction costs.

TRANSACTION COSTS AND THE COASE THEOREM

Professor Richard Adelstein of Wesleyan University has provided perhaps the simplest classroom explanation of the effects of insignificant transaction costs on the allocation of resources. In this section, we follow his exposition, somewhat modified to serve the purpose of this book (Pejovich, 1998, pp. 9–19). The example is a simple one, but it hints at numerous new issues that are created, almost daily, by new technologies. Those issues are resolved either by legislators, who are inclined to explain their solutions in terms of social welfare, or by common law judges, who prefer to focus on defining property rights. The advantage of the latter is that, once property rights are defined, individuals are free to seek to resolve conflicting interests via voluntary contracts.

Consider an example. Hamilton and Jefferson are neighbors. Their homes are next to each other. Hamilton and Jefferson value their homes at 1200 and 1000 euros, respectively. Those are subjective values indicating the prices at which Hamilton and Jefferson would sell their homes.[1] One day, Jefferson gets an offer from a company producing sirens to test their product in his kitchen. In exchange for his trouble, the company offers 500 euros. As Jefferson is hard of hearing, he gladly accepts the offer, which raises the subjective value of his home to 1500 euros. Of course, testing sirens imposes a subjective cost on Hamilton, which he values at, say, 200 euros. Thus, the values Jefferson and Hamilton place on their homes in the two situations are as shown in Table 2.1.

Table 2.1   The Coase theorem

	Hamilton	Jefferson	Total value
No sirens	1200 euros	1000 euros	2200 euros
Sirens	1000 euros	1500 euros	2500 euros

Hamilton believes that he has the right to be protected from the cacophony imposed on him by the testing of sirens in Jefferson's kitchen. Jefferson believes that he has the right to test sirens in his own home. Being unable to resolve the issue, Hamilton takes Jefferson to court.

It is assumed here that testing sirens in Jefferson's home has created a new issue that has not arisen before. The issue can be formalized as *the right of ownership in the noise from testing sirens*. In effect, the court has to decide who owns this right. Once the decision is made, this right, like all other private property rights, becomes transferable. The court's assignment of property rights in the noise from sirens enables Jefferson and Hamilton to resolve their conflict of interests contractually.

Suppose Hamilton wins. Initially there will be no sirens. However, the relevant property right is now defined. In the pursuit of his self-interest, Jefferson is willing to purchase from Hamilton the right to continue testing sirens. While he does not know the value Hamilton places on that right, Jefferson has incentives to keep raising his offer until a deal is made or the offer reaches 500 euros. In our example, at some price between 200 euros and 500 euros, exchange will happen. Suppose Jefferson buys the right for 300 euros. Then, the exchange between Hamilton and Jefferson has the following outcome: sirens are tested. The joint value of two homes is maximized at 2500 euros. Jefferson's share is 1300 euros, while Hamilton gets 1200 euros. The increment of 300 euros is shared by Hamilton and Jefferson; Jefferson gets 200 euros and Hamilton gets 100 euros.

Suppose Jefferson wins. Initially there are sirens. Driven by his self-interest, Hamilton has incentives to offer up to 200 euros to buy the right from Jefferson. However, Jefferson would accept no less than 500 euros. With no opportunity for exchange between Hamilton and Jefferson, we have the following outcome: sirens are tested. The joint value of two homes is maximized at 2500 euros. Jefferson's share is 1500 euros, while Hamilton ends up with 1000 euros. Jefferson captures the entire increment of wealth (300 euros). In addition, 200 euros are transferred from Hamilton to Jefferson.

The sirens are tested regardless of the initial allocation of the relevant property right, and the total value is maximized at 2500 euros either way. Only the distribution of this maximized value differs from one initial allocation to another. Hence, the Coase theorem: *Where bargaining is relatively costless, the process of exchange will bring about an efficient allocation of the relevant property right (i.e., the one that maximizes the value of production) regardless of the initial allocation of that right.*

The theorem makes two important points of far-reaching economic consequences: (1) clearly defined private property rights are an essential requirement for resolving the conflict of interests among individuals via market exchange, and (2) an efficient allocation of resources is independent of the initial assignment of property rights as long as transaction costs are insignificant.

However, the world of insignificant transaction costs *is not a Coasian world*. Coase's purpose was to persuade his colleagues to devote their energies to better understanding of the world of bounded rationality, and, in that world, the relevant choice for policy is not between two or more frictionless models but between two or more discrete institutional arrangements with positive transaction costs.

If transaction costs were positive and significant (in our example just a notch over 300 euros) the outcome of the dispute between Jefferson and Hamilton would depend on who got the right to decide whether the sirens are tested. If Hamilton won, Jefferson could not afford to buy the right to test sirens. In that case, the joint value of two homes would remain 2200 euros. An exchange opportunity would remain unexploited. However, if the judge assigned the right to test sirens to Jefferson, the value of the two homes would be maximized at 2500 euros.

It would be unrealistic to expect that initial assignment of property rights in new issues would necessarily go to individuals who value them most; that is, to individuals who would have bought those rights in the world of zero transaction costs (Jefferson, in our case). In a world of positive transaction costs, we can only look for incentives that would encourage the search for more efficient assignments of property rights in new issues. The book is about the search for such incentives.

Basic economic concepts

THE MAGNITUDE OF TRANSACTION COSTS

Transaction costs are part of the total costs of producing and exchanging goods and services. This means that the process of production and exchange necessitates positive production and transaction costs. Similarly, growing economies necessitate higher transaction and production costs.

John Wallis and Douglass North (1986) made the first comprehensive effort to develop a method for measuring transaction costs. Then they used the method they developed to provide the first empirical estimates of transaction costs in the United States economy for the period from 1870 to 1970. As in all innovative works, the study raised more questions than it answered. Hence, the study should be considered merely as a point of departure for further research (Table 2.2).

Table 2.2   The transaction costs as a percentage of GNP in the USA

Year	Private sector	Public sector	Total
1870	22.49	3.60	26.09
1880	25.27	3.60	28.87
1890	29.12	3.60	32.72
1900	30.43	3.67	34.10
1910	31.51	3.66	35.17
1920	35.10	4.87	39.98
1930	38.19	8.17	46.35
1940	37.09	6.60	43.69
1950	40.30	10.95	51.25
1960	41.30	14.04	55.35
1970	40.80	13.90	54.71

Source: Wallis and North (1986, p. 121).

The United States economy was more productive in the 1970s than in 1870s. The estimated increase in transaction costs does not mean that the economy has become less efficient. North and Wallis identified three reasons for the expansion of transaction costs: (1) economic development increases the extent of impersonal exchange, and this increase in the extent of impersonal exchange requires more information-gathering activity as well as more elaborate enforcement mechanisms;[2] (2) as new technology provides incentives for business firms to increase their operations, companies have to devote more resources to monitoring the process of production; (3) economic growth tends to raise questions about the justice and fairness of the distribution of wealth and income (income constituting the increment in wealth). Whether those conflicts emerge from differences in customs, race, ideology and/or loss of personalized relationships among individuals in the community, more resources have to be devoted to defining and enforcing the rules of the game.

The bottom line is that an increase of transaction costs is necessary in order to support more exchange, and thus more growth. That is, additional resources have to be used in order to realize the economic gains from unexploited exchange opportunities as well as to create new ones. An important analytical issue, then, is to identify the factors that affect changes in transaction costs and the circumstances upon which those factors depend.

WHY ARE TRANSACTION COSTS POSITIVE?

Simple examples are useful in helping us to understand the economic forces at work. Suppose Juventus and Chelsea are playing an important soccer game in London. The game is sold out and hundreds of people, including two faculty members at the London School of Economics, Winston and Margaret, have not been able to buy tickets. Their colleague, Tony, was lucky. He got one ticket at the selling price of 100 pounds.

During the week before the match, Winston and Margaret keep complaining about not being able to buy tickets. At some point, Tony tells them he would sell his ticket if the price were right or one of his colleagues offers to buy it. The sequence is of no consequence because the outcome should be the same. The important thing is that the value Tony and his two colleagues attach to watching the game is subjective and is not mutually known to them interpersonally. The only fact they all know is that Tony values the game at least as much as a bundle of other goods that 100 pounds could buy. Otherwise, he would not have purchased the ticket. They have no idea that watching the game is worth to Tony as much as a bundle of other goods that costs 130 pounds. Margaret and Winston also know that the maximum they are willing to pay for a ticket is 145 and 160 pounds, respectively.

Pursuing their respective self interest, Margaret offers a notch below 145 pounds. She drops out of the market when Winston offers, say, 150 pounds. If Tony were to accept Winston's offer, the message would be that the satisfaction Tony expects to get from spending 150 pounds on other goods exceeds the satisfaction from watching the Juventus–Chelsea game. If Tony were to accept Margaret's offer, the message would be that his total satisfaction – which would consist of 145 pounds in cash plus the nonpecuniary income of making a woman colleague happy – exceeds the satisfaction from selling the ticket to Winston for 150 pounds.

When the actors know one another well, the freedom to bid for scarce goods eventually reveals the subjective preferences of interacting individuals at low transaction costs, and the goods end up in the hands of those who value them the most. However, the final allocation of the ticket for the Juventus–Chelsea game might have been different had Tony known that someone from another section of the city was willing to pay 180 pounds to watch the game. With positive transaction costs, the process of voluntary exchange stops short of allocating goods to their highest-valued uses.

The real world is full of observations that the process of voluntary exchange stops short of allocating goods to their highest-valued uses. A young statistician looking for work might fail to learn about a job in another city, a housewife might not know about a lower price for beef in another store, and a visiting professor at the University of London might miss information about an empty apartment that is tailor-made for his needs. In all these cases some exchange opportunities are left unexploited and, because information is costly, the goods do not end up in the highest-valued uses. It is also costly to enter into exchange with individuals we have never met and/or with individuals whose customs and laws we do not know.

Unexploited opportunities for exchange mean forgone economic gains. To realize those potential gains, individuals have incentives to invest in producing information, reducing the costs of negotiating exchange, making the enforcement of contracts credible, and preventing opportunistic behavior. Indeed, we observe numerous activities aimed at increasing the extent of exchange, such as advertising, standardized contracts, and rules against opportunistic behavior.[3] Further, activities that reduce transaction costs increase the extent of exchange. Major sources of positive transaction costs, then, are the cost of information, the costs of negotiating exchange, the costs of monitoring exchange, the costs of enforcing exchange, the costs of accepting the risk of exchange, and the cost of maintaining the rule of law.

SOURCES OF POSITIVE TRANSACTION COSTS

Positive transaction costs can be imposed by the state or another authority, or they can be a consequence of bounded rationality. The former are also called exogenous transaction costs, while the latter are referred to as endogenous transaction costs.

Exogenous Transaction Costs

Suppose that reselling tickets for the Chelsea–Juventus game is subject to a sales tax of 35 pounds. We recall that Tony values the ticket as much as 130 pounds' worth of other goods. With a sales tax of 35 pounds, the minimum price he will accept is a notch over 165 pounds.

With this increase in the transaction costs of buying tickets, Tony will not be able to sell his ticket to Winston. A sales tax – or any other formal rule increasing the transaction costs of exchange (i.e., price controls, restricted sales on Sundays, etc) – creates a restraint on trade that the system cannot alleviate from within. The extent of exchange may (and often does) increase via black market activities, but, owing to their higher risk and transaction costs, black markets are not likely to maximize the extent of exchange.

A sales tax of, say, 20 pounds would not interfere with the allocation of resources; that is, Tony would sell the ticket to Winston for below 160 pounds. In this case, the difference between having a tax and having no tax would affect only the allocation of income between individuals and the state. However, ours is a simple, one-exchange, one-game (activity) example. In the real world, with a large number of buyers in the market for oversold games, the extent of exchange would be reduced because some buyers would not be willing to pay a premium in excess of 20 pounds. In general, any exogenously imposed increase in transaction costs restricts the extent of exchange.

The example is not very realistic. It is hard to imagine a sales tax on reselling tickets for oversold soccer games. The example, does, however, make a point that is relevant for discussion of the causes and effects of transaction costs. Chelsea is a privately owned club. Why would its owner or manager (hereafter: the owner) fail to charge the market clearing price? Ignorance of market conditions is not an answer. Chelsea is playing major matches all the time and the owner should have rather a good understanding of the demand for tickets at different times and for different games. Two answers consistent with the owner's self-interest are (a) selling tickets below the market clearing price reduces the club's total receipts. However, the resulting excess demand for tickets creates the perception that Chelsea is a very popular club with huge demand for tickets; and (b) the shortage of tickets means that the owner has something of value that cannot be purchased in the open market.

With the shortage of tickets, the owner has a very valuable good to ration. He can trade tickets for nonpecuniary favors up to the point where the satisfaction from nonpecuniary favors becomes equal to the revenue lost per ticket. A cardiologist would have a better chance of getting a ticket than would a retired professor; a member of parliament would have a better chance than a secretary, the CEO of a large local firm would have a better chance than a blue-collar worker, and a plumber (we all need them occasionally) would have a better chance than a homely widow.

Endogenous Transaction Costs

Suppose that a person residing somewhere in London is willing to pay as much as 180 pounds for a ticket. Unfortunately, Tony and that person are not aware of each other. Consequently, the ticket goes to Winston for any price between the 145 pounds offered by Margaret and 160 pounds, which is the maximum Winston is willing to pay for the right to watch the game. Positive transaction costs prevent the ticket from moving to its highest valued use. In the case of endogenous transaction costs, a remedy is available from within the system.

Tony has a student who does not care much about football but is eager to make money. He enters the bargaining game and buys the ticket from Tony (or from Winston if Winston has already bought it from Tony) for a notch above 160 pounds. Clearly, the student is willing to take the risk of finding a soccer fan willing to pay a sum high enough to cover the costs of the ticket, the transaction cost of finding the buyer, and a residual. Looking for a buyer, the student can choose among many strategies, such as advertising in local papers, going online, visiting sporting events and standing at the entrance to the stadium before the game. All those strategies require the expenditure of the student's time (i.e., the opportunity costs of his labor) and some direct expenses.

If the student succeeds in his efforts and sells the ticket at a price above 160 pounds, Tony and the buyer would be better off than before the trade. As for the student, the difference between 160 pounds and the price at which he sells the ticket is his return. The return includes two elements: what is necessary to cover the (transaction) costs of finding the buyer and an entrepreneurial reward. The student bears the risk of failing to find a buyer at a price higher than what he paid for the ticket. Indeed, we observe scalpers having to sell tickets for various sporting and musical events below their costs. In these cases they incur a loss. We can say that free and unrestricted exchange (i.e., the right to resell tickets at any price the market will bear) generates incentives for individuals to incur transaction costs necessary for additional exchange to occur. It is efficiency-friendly.

The analysis can be extended from an individual like the student in our example to the behavior of business firms. They also have incentives to reduce transaction costs. For example, given its standard method of production and quality control, Dell discovers that one out of every thousand computers is defective. Dell has two major ways of reducing the number of defective computers per 1000 it produces. The company can spend additional resources on inspecting computers before they leave the factory, or the company can shift the costs of identifying defective units to a lower cost provider of such information, namely, the consumer. Dell can do this by offering all sorts of warranties, guarantees and return privileges to consumers (one out of a thousand) whose computers turn out to be defective. The company is better off because it does not have to invest additional resources in the inspection of each and every unit it produces. And the buyers of Dell computers are better off: they are better off because they get computers at a lower price relative to what the price would have been if additional resources were used to reduce the number of defective units.

The examples of Tony's student and Dell capture the essence of the world in which we live. In pursuing their self-interest, real estate agents, employment agencies, scalpers, business firms and all other organizations and individuals engage in activities that minimize the increases in transaction costs necessary to support a larger volume of production and exchange. An unintended consequence of their 'selfish' pursuits is more efficient economy. To pursue those efficiency-producing activities, individuals and organizations must have incentives, and the rules of the game shape those incentives. Thus, to understand differences in economic performance between countries requires analysis of the effects of alternative institutional arrangements on transaction costs.

NOTES

1. Realistic numbers would make the exposition more complex to follow. The same goes for distinguishing between the stock-values of homes and the flow of benefits per unit of time. The purpose here is to present Coase's theorem as simply as possible without affecting its message.
2. The simplest explanation is as follows: a Freiburg merchant in the Middle Ages trades locally and makes a weekly profit of two golden coins. He could increase profit to four golden coins by taking his merchandise to Basel, except that the road to Basel is insecure; that is, the transaction costs are too high (higher than two golden coins). If the local lord were able to guarantee the secure passage, he could charge a tax of up to two golden coins. We can interpret the outcome in two ways, both of which are correct. First, we can say that a decrease in transaction costs of shipping goods to Basel from over four to below two golden coins increased the extent of exchanges (and the total value of output), making more exchange possible. Second, we can say that positive transaction costs of less than two golden coins are necessary to increase the extent of exchange (and the total value of output).
3. For example, the rule forbidding New York transit employees to strike during the busy Christmas season.

REFERENCES

Coase, R. (1988), *The Firm, the Market, and the Law*, Chicago: University of Chicago Press.

Pejovich, S. (1998), *Economic Analysis of Institutions and Systems*, Dordrecht: Kluwer Academic Publishers (revised 2nd edn).

Wallis, J. and D. North (1986), 'Measuring the transaction sector in the United States economy, 1870–1970', in S. Engerman and R. Gallman (eds), *Long-Term Factors in American Economic Growth*, Chicago: University Of Chicago Press, pp. 95–161.

PART II

Transformation of the medieval community into
modern society: the rise of classical liberalism,
the rule of law and capitalism

3.   From the Middle Ages to capitalism

The collapse of the Roman Empire eliminated both Roman law, which was based on private ownership and contracts, and the machinery that enforced it. When the Germanic tribes, collectively known as the barbarians, took power in Rome towards the end of the fifth century AD, their customs replaced Roman law. Given the nomadic background of the Germanic tribes, the Germans held the notion of private property as less important than the preservation and development of group solidarity. Thus, incentives were in place for the development of new social arrangements.

A survival strategy for a weaker man was to turn to a stronger man and give the latter nontransferable right of ownership in his land in exchange for protection and an inalienable right of tenancy: the right to hold the land of the lord. This relationship, which was named the lord–vassal relationship, slowly evolved into a basic social institution in medieval Europe. A lord could and often did become the vassal of still another man; that is, he became both the lord of a weaker man and the vassal of a stronger man. The king was at the top of this chain, and the actual tillers of the land (serfs) were at the bottom.

The Catholic Church (hereafter, the Church) provided cultural unity to a politically fragmented Western Europe. In addition to monopoly in the market for salvation, the Church also had monopoly in the market for knowledge.[1] To secure the former, the Church relied on persecution of heretics, inquisition, threat of damnation, and crusades. As for the latter, libraries were located in monasteries and cathedrals, and the vast majority of literate people were monks. These monopolies provided incentives for the Church to shape the development of the first post-Roman government institutions, bureaucracy, and a judiciary. Consequently, the Church had considerable influence in the development of informal rules of the game in the Middle Ages (Ekelund et al., 1996, p. 182).

Eventually, a new socioeconomic system developed in the post-Roman vacuum. It was based on a hierarchy of individuals holding specific, largely nontransferable, property rights in land and two main pillars. One was the old Roman-style political structure, whereby a stronger man would secure loyalties from more valuable weaker men by dispensing *honores*. The second pillar was a loose legal order based on a mix of religious and customary rules. The uniqueness of the system rested on its pseudo-contractual rights in land, which, coupled with the scarcity of labor, provided all social classes, and especially peasants, with protection from arbitrary decision of kings, princes and bishops.

An important step in weakening this early period of Middle Ages was taken by Charles the Bald (833–877), who allowed the nobles to transfer to their children the privileges originally granted through the *honores*. As a result, the aristocracy started to evolve from being a class of individuals co-opted by the prince and personally dependent on the prince's benevolence into a group of privileged local rulers legitimized by birth. The military or administrative aristocracy quickly became the elite among land owners.

Another important step was taken at the end of the eleventh century by Pope Gregory vii. The pope declared that the clergy must be free from secular control. Instead, he ordained that kings and lords ruled by the grace of God rather than with the consent of their subjects. The Gregorian revolution created two parallel jurisdictions, secular and ecclesiastical, sparking in many parts of Europe a legal transformation that benefited all other social classes, including the serfs. To various degrees, civil law (Venice), urban law (Italian municipalities) and the law merchant (almost everywhere) are good examples of the successful institutional arrangements that followed, all of which contributed to creating secure rights and enhancing trade.[2]

Yet the Middle Ages failed to produce fast growth and high living standards for at least two reasons. First, medieval banks failed to create bank credit. According to Josef Schumpeter, this failure of the banking system was a major reason that the development of early capitalism in Italian cities such as Genoa and Venice could not have been sustained.[3] Second, only in the eighteenth century did the gradual rise in agricultural productivity reach the tipping point where it became profitable to link technological innovation with entrepreneurship, ultimately leading to extensive mechanization. And only in the nineteenth century did transportation costs fall dramatically, thereby opening up virtually unlimited markets (and rewards to entrepreneurial endeavors).

PHILOSOPHICAL FOUNDATIONS OF CAPITALISM

The two cornerstones of capitalism are classical liberalism and methodological individualism. Individualism means that human action is the result of emotions, desires, preferences and evaluations that only the individual can develop and appreciate. Decisions made by governments, parliaments, corporations and other organizations are actually decisions made by individuals. Individuals conceive ideas, invest time and effort in formulating policies, convince others to accept their ideas and bear the risk of failures.

The source of individualism in the West can be traced to Christianity. The focus of Christianity is on the individual and the individual's relation to God who created individuals, not collectives. A direct link between the individual and God posits that each individual is endowed with the knowledge of what is good for himself or herself and with the ability to choose. Eventually the Enlightenment, the French Revolution, socialism and many other ideologies have replaced the concept of individual liberty with that of a common good defined by the elite running the state and/or representing various ideologies, yet the concept of individualism has survived to our days, except that God has largely been left out. The Chicago School and Austrian economics, to mention two major intellectual movements in the West, have successfully continued to present analytical and empirical evidence that our understanding of the economic forces at work requires that we consider the individual as the unit of analysis.

The culture of individualism rewards competitive performance, promotes risk taking and views income inequalities as desirable results of entrepreneurship and free trade. It sees the community as a voluntary association of individuals who, in the pursuit of their private ends, join and leave the community by free choice. Holding the individual to be superior to any group encourages behavior based on the principles of *self-interest, self-responsibility* and *self-determination.* And those principles of behavior rest on informal rules to which this book refers interchangeably as the culture of individualism and the culture of capitalism. Geoffrey Hodgson (2007) argues that, by emphasizing the relationship between individuals, methodological individualism provides room for the introduction of institutional arrangements into economic analysis.

We can trace the philosophical foundations of classical liberalism – the second cornerstone of capitalism – to the writings of great thinkers from the fifteenth to eighteenth centuries, such as John Locke, David Hume, Bernard Mandeville and Adam Smith.[4] Unlike the thinkers of the Middle Ages who considered the universe as constant and eternal, new generations of scholars began to realize that human history is an endless evolution of social institutions. As a footnote, it is important to note that we should attribute the resurrection of classical liberalism in the second half of the twentieth century to a number of scholars, including Milton Friedman, James Buchanan, Bruno Leoni and Friedrich Hayek.

Classical liberalism is about individual liberty, openness to new ideas, tolerance of all views, private property rights, the rule of law and the freedom of contracts. Individual liberty, openness to new ideas and tolerance of the values held by others create an environment in which individuals are free to pursue their private ends. In a classical liberal society individuals are expected to tolerate one another's preferences, while the state is expected to protect those preferences from external interference (including by the state itself).

A major step in the development of classical liberalism was the fifteenth-century revival of interest in the cultural heritage of Rome and Greece. The heritage of Rome was a legal system, which emphasized private property rights and the law of commerce. The heritage of Greece was inquisitive reasoning, which is a springboard for the development of science. Predictably, the revival of interest in the cultural tradition of Rome and Greece triggered the emergence of powerful new ideas.

However, the development of classical liberalism and individualism has taken different paths in England and Continental Europe. In a very interesting study, Russell Hardin asked why the two liberalisms differ (1993). One reason, he argued, is that liberalism in England, for reasons that are beyond the purpose of this book, was more interested in piecemeal resolution of social issues via voluntary interactions among freely choosing individuals, while liberalism in Continental Europe was more in tune with collective rulings on social issues. And those different paths have made a major contribution to today's capitalism in the United Kingdom and North America, on the one hand, and on the European continent, on the other.

INDIVIDUALISM AND CLASSICAL LIBERALISM IN ENGLAND

Alan Macfarlane (1979) traced the birth of individualism in England to the thirteenth century. He describes the individualism of that time as follows: 'Society is constituted of autonomous equal units, namely separate individuals. ... It is reflected in the concept of individual property, in the political and legal liberty of the individual, in the idea of the individual's direct communication with God' (p. 196).

It is possible to trace the development of classical liberalism in England to numerous sources, such as the replication of the lessons and successes of mercantile capitalism typical of Italy and then of the Netherlands; the influence of great thinkers of the seventeenth and eighteenth centuries; the adoption of common law; and the absence of a strong king. The important fact is that classical liberalism did happen in England at a time when new formal rules subsumed local traditions and, in doing so, enhanced the emergence of secure contracts, credible property rights and protection of individual wealth in England (North and Weingast, 1989). As a consequence the extent of exchange increased.

While West Europeans (mostly Portuguese and Spaniards) took medieval institutions with them to South and Central America, most settlers came to North America to escape them. Settlers had a 'rebellious' desire to make their own choices, choose their own morals, and develop their own rules of the game. Thus, people who went to North America saw and treated new frontiers as a tradition-free space.

The tradition-free space in North America allowed the settlers to pursue their individual preferences; to take the responsibility for their own actions; to retain some traditional customs and drop others, to develop new rules; and in general to create their own way of life based on the principles of self-interest, self-responsibility and self-determination.[5] The exploration and settlement of North America had then an unintended consequence of strengthening as well as modifying the classical liberalism of England.

Not surprisingly, Anglo-American liberalism harbors a strong dose of skepticism about the rulers' foresight and their goodwill. It is in tune with formal rules that provide individuals with the freedom to pursue their private ends and to enter into contractual agreements with one another. The Anglo-American tradition considers that the primary function of formal rules is to support the objectives of interacting individuals rather than to seek specific outcomes. Anglo-American capitalism is the institutionalized version of the classical liberalism of England.

INDIVIDUALISM AND CLASSICAL LIBERALISM IN WESTERN EUROPE

The Continental tradition rests on two assumptions: (1) there exists a just society, and (2) human reason is capable of discovering the formal rules required to bring about such a society. These two assumptions of the Continental tradition provided both the philosophical raison d'être for the academic community to support social engineering, and the political justification for governments to pursue it.

This is not to say that individualism and classical liberalism failed to reach Western Europe. They did. However, the development of individualism and classical liberalism in continental Western Europe had a few bumps. Absolute monarchies and the French Revolution did away with most medieval traditions. Parallel jurisdictions of the Middle Ages slowly gave way to the expansion of central secular powers. Legislators and autocrats took over the enactment of new formal laws.

The contributions of intellectuals like Montesquieu or Galiani remained relatively isolated and were overshadowed by the triumphant French Enlightenment, which failed to establish roots in England (and later North America). Montesquieu was well aware of the great economic liberties enjoyed in England in the early part of the eighteenth century; in the seventeenth century the fourth Earl of Shaftsbury had formulated similar remarks with respect to the Netherlands. The difference was that England followed the Dutch example, while France remained a centralized, territorial power.

The French Revolution of 1789 was not carried out in the name of the individual. It was carried out in the name of a new concept of legitimate centralism enforced by an 'enlightened' ruling elite. All this was not swept away by the

Restoration, for the aftermath of the Napoleonic Era continued to be characterized less by individual liberties and much more by powerful nationalism.

Contrary to the English and American experiences, the role of a powerful state has never been seriously questioned on the European continent, not even by its most prominent classical liberals. They accepted the state as the watchdog of all individual actions, including those in the economic domain: 'The economic system cannot be left to organize itself' (Eucken, 1951, p. 93), for 'undiluted capitalism is intolerable' (Roepke, 1958, p. 119).

THE DEVELOPMENT OF COMMON LAW AND CIVIL LAW

Two different legal systems, common law and civil law, emerged from classical liberalism in England and Europe. In common law, judges play a crucial role in developing as well as in maintaining the legal system. Judges do this by formalizing customs and traditions that have already been agreed upon, and by creating new rules when it is necessary to meet the changing requirements of social and economic life (the case in Chapter 2 of the noise from sirens is an oversimplified example). And when the parties belong to different communities, common law judges are expected to enforce the rules that apply in a given trade. Common law is also called judge-made law.

In a civil law system, the legislators have incentives to enact formal rules that reflect their perceptions of the preferences of the median voter. The task of judges in civil law countries is to appreciate the meaning of those rules, interpret them and adapt them to the (unforeseen) circumstances if and when necessary. Their main function is not to make rules but to interpret and enforce the rules enacted by legislators.

The basic difference between the two systems, then, lies in the roles they assign to the legislators and judges. In comparison with civil law countries, legislators in common law states are relatively less important, especially when the courts have the right of judicial review, as in the United States. For centuries the English Parliament was not interested in what we think of today as 'ordinary law making'; Parliament's chief concern lay in granting or denying the king permission to levy taxation, in most cases in order to wage war. Yet, driven by their self-interest, the legislators in common law countries have been increasing their relative importance by intrusion of statutes and government regulations into the system. That is what has been happening in the United States, beginning with the New Deal in the 1930s.

We can say that legislators and judges in common law and civil law countries have different incentives. As we shall see in Chapter 13, those incentives inevitably have an impact on the formation as well as the development of formal rules.

Common Law

The Magna Carta of 1215 and the Glorious Revolution of 1688–89 made major contributions to the weakening of central power in England. While absolute monarchies were rising in Europe, England was de facto ruled by the landed aristocracy and the emerging middle class. This dispersion of power did not imply the absence of law and order, for the enactment and enforcement of laws do not require a centralized authority (Benson, 1989, p. 49). For instance, the law merchant, development of which goes back to the eleventh century, antedates the emergence of nation-states. The development of the law merchant led to the reduction of the costs of exchange and the protection of foreign merchants against exploitation by local rules. The development of private property rights in the American West during the nineteenth century (through homesteading and the closing of the open ranges) reduced the transaction costs of exchange.

By the end of the seventeenth century, the law merchant was not the only legal system to which litigants could refer. For instance, the crown had its own system (the King's Bench, which subsequently became known as the common law) and people were free to choose. Sir Edward Coke, a leading advocate of the common law system, introduced a number of innovations that attracted more cases to common law courts and finally made common law the prevailing system. By the end of the eighteenth century, the transition to the common law was complete. Common law judges became open and flexible enough to absorb many features of the law merchant. The development of common law has then strengthened the protection of free trade and private property rights.

Appellate common law judges were empowered to reverse decisions rendered by both lower common law courts and merchant courts, and procedures were codified to reduce judiciary discretion. The basic principle of common law, *stare decisis*, which in Latin means 'stand by things decided', was fully accepted. Stare decisis says that a judge has to apply the law as it is presented through the previous decisions of the court. By implication, the common law is the institutionalization of informal institutions.

The fact that common law replaced the law merchant provides a key insight into the virtues of the Anglo-American institutional framework. As the extent of exchange increased within communities and between them, common law outcompeted the law merchant by reducing the transaction costs of enforcement, and by being more credible and predictable. The argument for the lower transaction costs of common law said that the law merchant 'in each recurring case, have to enter upon its examination and decision as if all were new, without any aid from the experience of the past, or the benefit of any established principle or settled law. Each case … would in turn pass away and be forgotten, leaving behind it no record of principle established, or light to guide, or rule to govern the future' (*Hanford* v. *Archer*, 4 Hill, 321). To state matters plainly, at some stage of economic development, common law did a better job than the law merchant in reducing the transaction costs of resolving conflicts among interacting individuals.

Moreover, the common law was in tune with the rising individualism in England. The source of its legitimacy was local traditions and customs; that is, informal rules. And this tie to the rising individualism and informal institutions explains an important trait of common law up to the beginning of the twenty-first century. Common law is not about social justice, welfare or collective ends; it is about individual liberty, private property rights and free exchange.

William Blackstone (1765–69) played the major role in defining procedures to be used by common law judges in accepting customs as precedents (1765, p. 69). A critical decision was made in 1833 (*Mirehouse* v. *Rennell*, IC1&F., 527, 546). It defined the relationship between customs, law and changing conditions of life as follows:

> Our Common Law system consists in the applying to new combinations of circumstances those rules which we derive from legal principles and judicial precedent; and for the sake of attaining uniformity, consistency, and certainty, we must apply those rules, where they are not plainly unreasonable and inconvenient, to all cases which arise; and we are not at liberty to reject them, and to abandon all analogy to them, in those to which they have not yet been judicially applied, because we think that the rules are not as convenient and reasonable as we ourselves could have devised. It appears to me to be of great importance to keep this principle of decision steady in view, not merely for the determination of the particular case, but for the interests of law as a science.

A precedent is a reason for deciding a similar case the same way, yet economic and social developments make precedents obsolete, and obsolete precedents need to be replaced (Posner, 2003, ch. 20). Regarding the overturning of precedents, Benson wrote (Benson, 2005): 'In *Prah* v. *Maretti* the judge ruled that 'Courts should not implement obsolete policies that have lost their vigor over the course of the years ... Clearly, courts can follow precedent and explicitly state that they are bound to do so ... they can also legislate new law and explicitly acknowledge that they are overturning precedent.'

These two cases, *Prah* v. *Maretti* and *Mirehouse* v. *Rennell*, suggest that common law judges can choose either to stick with the prevailing precedents or to ignore them and 'legislate from the bench'. An implication is that judges have discretionary power to make decisions that are not consistent with either the wisdom of the past or existing precedents. The extent of their discretionary power depends on judges' incentives and external constraints, which are discussed in Chapter 13.

Civil Law

In civil law countries, scholars conceptualize their perceptions of a just or better society into legal propositions and/or legal doctrines. Legislators debate the propositions and enact those that pass their scrutiny. Finally, bureaucrats and courts implement and enforce new formal rules. The German version of capitalism, known as the Social Market Economy, is perhaps the most obvious economic consequence of the continental legal tradition (Barry, 1993).

The formal rules enacted by legislators are directly influenced by the people and groups who expect to be affected by those rules, one way or another. Suppose the city of Birmingham is considering a subsidy for the arts, which would include the museum, symphony and a major gallery, all of them consumption goods. The annual cost of the subsidy is estimated at $10 million per year. To finance the project, 500 000 city taxpayers would have to pay a fixed annual tax of $20 per taxpayer.

Suppose that 10 000 taxpayers would spend $250 each per year to enjoy the satisfaction from activities that the subsidy is to make available to them in exchange for a $20 tax. Their total benefits from the subsidy, adjusted for the tax of $20, would be $2 300 000 per year or $230 per person. The remaining 490 000 taxpayers would not spend any money at all on enjoying arts. The subsidy is then economically inefficient. First, it interferes with the right of 490 000 taxpayers who do not care about culture to spend $20 per year on the goods they prefer. Second, the 'culture lovers' get a free ride at other people's expense. An efficiency-friendly alternative is to let the people of Birmingham have as much culture as they are willing to pay for, yet inefficient rules are frequently approved by legislators (in this case by an elected city council). Why?

Given their expected benefits, 10 000 taxpayers have incentives to invest up to $230 to convince their elected council that Birmingham should subsidize arts. Those taxpayers who do not care about museums, classical music and great paintings have incentives to invest only up to or about $20 per person to prevent the rule from being enacted. The former are a small group with high individual stakes in getting the subsidy enacted. Their transaction costs of organizing and lobbying are relatively low. The latter are a large group with low individual stakes in stopping the subsidy. They could easily discover that the transaction costs of organizing and preventing a bad rule from being enacted is in excess of a tax of $20. In real life, the spread between the benefits captured by few and the costs borne by all is then an important factor affecting the enactment of formal rules.

Moreover, the legislative process creates a valuable property right for legislators. They have the power to confer gains and to impose costs on individuals. The legislative process, then, creates a 'market of sorts' for formal rules in which legislators are trading favors in exchange for support and campaign contributions. Indeed, we observe that various rent-seeking coalitions (e.g., trade unions, business establishments) are active in this market.[6] A major constraint on legislators' discretionary power is the probability that the median voter might react negatively to their behavior.

The process does not provide incentives for legislators to avoid passing inefficient rules. However, it is wrong to blame rent-seeking coalitions for the resulting economic inefficiencies, when the real source of those inefficiencies is the ability of rule-makers in office to use political power to reward some voters and penalize others. The Nobel laureate, George Stigler (1971, p. 3) wrote: 'The state is a potential resource or threat to every industry in the society. With its power to prohibit or compel, to take or give money, the state can and does selectively help or hurt a vast number of industries.'

IS THE CONVERGENCE OF TWO LEGAL SYSTEMS LIKELY?

Is competition between the two legal systems going to produce some kind of convergence or are they more likely to continue to diverge along their path dependency trajectories? The convergence thesis asserts that countries eventually select the most efficient legal rules. The path dependency thesis says that the choices countries make are constrained by the transaction costs of departing from the prevailing institutional framework.

Some scholars observe that common law countries are enacting statutes while civil law countries are adjusting their formal rules to local customs and traditions (Barry, 2004). They interpret those observations as steps towards the convergence of the two legal systems. Easterbrook and Fischel (1991) discuss the issue of corporate structure. They argue that competition between different legal rules will eventually select the most effective type of corporate governance.

It is more likely that what is seen as convergence of the two legal systems in fact reflects the importation from above of statutes and regulations into common law countries; that is, the apparent convergence represents a change in the mix of statutes and judge-made rules. The change in the mix of statutes and judge-made rules in favor of the former is usually justified in terms of social justice, the common good or social welfare, yet all those terms are arguably the façade of words hiding the self-interest of legislators seeking to increase their political power. Not only are terms like social justice or social welfare ambiguous and yet to be defined, but they crowd out common law precedents, which are protective of individual rights, private property and free exchange. There is therefore good reason to say that the infusion of statutes and government regulations into the legal system is not efficiency-friendly.

The argument for the two systems remaining on their own dependency path trajectories hinges on the significant transaction costs of merging the two systems. For instance, North (1990, p. 101) noted: 'The US Constitution was adopted with modifications by many Latin American countries in the nineteenth century, and many of the property rights laws of successful Western countries have been adopted by third world countries. The results are, however, not similar to those in the United States or other successful Western countries. The enforcement mechanism, the norms of behavior, and the subjective models of the actors are not [the same].'

The transaction costs of the convergence of two legal systems arise from the individual's perception of reality, which is shaped by the prevailing institutional framework and by the bargaining power of the interest groups that the system favors (e.g., German labor unions have been successful in defending labor participation in the management of business firms, or codetermination). Transaction costs are also affected by the costs of investment in the prevailing set of rules (sunk costs), the costs of maintaining the network of information-processing procedures, and the costs of enforcement.

NOTES

1. Martin Luther (1483–1546) and John Calvin (1509–64) bore the costs of opening up the market for salvation by offering a new interpretation of guidance to the attainment of redemption. Their respective interpretations of the product offered by Christianity passed the market test and the Catholic Church lost its monopoly in the market for guidance to the attainment of salvation. Moreover, the Church monopoly in the temporal world was weakened as well.
2. The law merchant is a private legal system developed by merchants in medieval Europe, including England.
3. The development of bank credit is traceable to 1797, when the British government forbade the bank to pay its notes in gold. This rule opened the door to a rapid increase in the volume of bank credit.
4. The term 'liberalism' has come to mean different things to different people. It certainly means two different things in the United States and Western Europe. For that reason, my reference to liberalism as classical liberalism is necessary.
5. The people who went to North America in the early days of the new frontiers were often referred to as criminal elements. Indeed, they were criminals by the then prevailing standards, when it was a crime to oppose the established order, reject medieval tradition, complain about the church and avoid taxes imposed by kings, feudal lords and bishops.
6. This analysis does not say that legislators are crooks; it merely says that legislators, like all other individuals, respond to incentives. Further, the analysis does not rule out the possibility that rules pushed through legislature by various pressure groups might turn out to be beneficial. All that the analysis in this section says is that the process under which legislators work does not have a built-in bias to seek and sustain efficient rules.

REFERENCES

Barry, N. (1993), 'The social market economy', *Social Philosophy and Policy*, **10**(2), 1–25.
Barry, N. (2004), 'Property rights in common and civil law', in E. Colombatto (ed.), *The*

Elgar Companion to the Economics of Property Rights, Cheltenham, UK and North-ampton, MA, USA: Edward Elgar, pp. 177–96.

Benson, B. (1989), 'The spontaneous evolution of commercial law', *Southern Economic Journal*, **55**(3), January, 644–61.

Benson, B. (2005), 'Common law versus judge made law', *Working Paper*, Florida.

Blackstone, W. (1765–69), *Commentaries on the Laws of England*, Oxford: Clarendon Press.

Easterbrook, F. and D. Fischel (1991), *The Economic Structure of Corporate Law*, Chicago: University of Chicago Press.

Ekelund, R. et al. (1996), *Sacred Trust: The Medieval Church as an Economic Firm*, Oxford: Oxford University Press.

Eucken, W. (1951), *The Unsuccessful Age*, Edinburgh: William Hodges.

Hardin, R (1993), 'Liberalism: political and economic', *Social Philosophy and Policy*, **10**(2), 121–44.

Hodgson, G. (2007), 'Meanings of methodological individualism', *Journal of Economic Methodology*, **14**(2), 211–26.

Macfarlane, A. (1979), *The Origins of English Individualism*, Oxford: Blackwell.

North, D. (1990), *Institutions, Institutional Change and Economic Performance,* Cambridge: Cambridge University Press.

North, D. and B. Weingast (1989), 'Constitutions and commitment: the evolution of institutions governing public choice in seventeenth-century England', *Journal of Economic History*, **49**(4), 803–32.

Posner, R. (2003), *Economic Analysis of Law*, New York: Aspen.

Roepke, W. (1958), *Social Crisis of Our Time*, London: Thames and Hudson.

Stigler, G. (1971), 'The theory of government regulation', *Bell Journal of Economics*, **2**(1), 3–21.

4. Capitalism and the rule of law

Capitalism is institutionalized classical liberalism. Its cornerstones are competitive markets, the rule of law and the culture of individualism. There is a great deal of literature on the transformation of feudalism to capitalism. As for the dating of capitalism, Schumpeter argued (1954, p. 78) that, by the end of the fifteenth century, most institutions and behaviors we associate with capitalism were already in place.

There is also a great deal of literature on the rise of capitalism. From the standpoint of this book, the most interesting debate is between Macfarlane and Weber. The former sees the origin of capitalism in the rise of individualism in thirteenth century England. Weber argued that the Puritan spirit emerging from Calvin's teaching gave tremendous impetus to the development of the frugal, hardworking and accumulating individual. Macfarlane wrote (1978, pp. 197–8): 'It is no longer possible to explain the origins of English individualism in terms of ... Protestantism ... If [capitalism] was present in 1250, it is clear that neither the spread of world trade and colonization, nor Protestantism, can have much to do with its origins.' If one accepted that individualism is the key element of capitalism, Macfarlane wins the argument. However, there is also an argument that both scholars could have been right because what Weber meant by capitalism was quite different from what Macfarlane meant (Opp 1983, pp. 28–30). Analysis in this book accepts Macfarlane's position that individualism is a major defining characteristic of capitalism.

The transformation of ideas and concepts into a real world system has positive transaction costs. Some of those transaction costs are endogenous to the system and are discussed throughout the book. Others are exogenous and come from the critics of capitalism and are briefly mentioned here.

Sir Thomas More (1478–1535) was the first significant critic of capitalism. He based his criticism on the moral teachings of the early Church fathers. While realizing that the world was changing, More argued that changes must be made within the bounds of the moral teachings of the church.

Early Catholic theologians and philosophers raised the issue of the legitimacy of capitalism as a moral system. They were apprehensive about freedom of choice, not because of any lack of interest in individual liberty but because of a fear that autonomy of individual choices in the free market does not necessarily generate morally satisfying sets of preferences. Yet the fact is that our values are formed in various places, such as homes, schools, churches, the streets, our friends, the media and the like, and are merely revealed in the free market. Suppressing freedom of choice does not change a person's morals. It merely deprives him of an opportunity to choose and bear the cost of his choice.

In the seventeenth and eighteenth centuries, early socialism flourished in France and eventually reached England and the rest of the European continent. The primary mission of early socialists was to eliminate the social and economic inequalities of the system. Having no appreciation for scarcity and opportunity costs, they advocated equality of results over equal opportunity to compete in free markets. As a way of accomplishing their goal of economic equality, early socialists directed their major criticism of capitalism at private property rights.

The twentieth century witnessed the rise of two major applications of the socialist doctrine: National Socialism and Marxism–Leninism. National Socialism and Marxism–Leninism shared many basic political and economic premises of the socialist doctrine. They both ran command economies. They made the individual a bare tool in the achievement of the ends of their ruling elites. National Socialism and Marxism–Leninism were hostile to capitalism, and its corollary, the society of free and responsible individuals. They favored a large and active state, created comprehensive welfare programs, and paid no heed to the rule of law. National Socialism and Marxism–Leninism had some fundamental differences as well. Communists were openly hostile to the right of ownership, while national socialists were comfortable with controlling and monitoring the behavior of private owners. National socialists saw the struggle for racial purity within national boundaries as the major mechanism for the development of their brand of socialism. Communists, on the other hand, saw the class struggle waged by the proletariat across national boundaries as the vehicle for the development of the Marxist–Leninist type of socialism. The Second World War destroyed Hitler's socialism from without. Marxism–Leninism decayed from within.

Unlike other systems that have been tried, capitalism has survived the test of time; it has passed the economic efficiency test. Adam Smith described the new system, which he called the Natural System of Economic Liberty, as being self-generating, self-propelling and self-regulating. Some people have called it laissez-faire. Property rights scholars refer to it as the private property, free-market economy. Werner Sombart (1902) named it capitalism, and the name capitalism stuck. In this book, I use the terms *private-property, free-market economy* and *capitalism* interchangeably

Economic performance of the private-property, free-market economy depends on the incentive effects of the system's formal and informal institutions. And those institutions are neither the same from one capitalist country to another nor written in stone. To establish the relationship between capitalism and economic performance, the line of reasoning throughout the book is straightforward: institutions (formal and informal) create their own behavioral incentives. Different incentives have different effects on the transaction costs of exchange. Different transaction costs have different effects on the extent of exchange and the flow of innovation in the economy. And the extent of exchange and the flow of innovation are major determinants of economic performance.

A growing body of literature demonstrates a strong positive relationship between the incentive effects of the basic institutions of capitalism and economic performance. The Fraser Institute and the Heritage Foundation annually provide empirical evidence that confirms this relationship. In defining economic freedom, both indexes use the categories that also define the free-market, private-property economy or capitalism. Mary Anastasia O'Grady (2007, p. 32), a co-editor of the *Index of Economic Freedom*, published jointly by the Heritage Foundation and *Wall Street Journal*, wrote: 'The world isn't only growing richer. The gap between the per-capita income of have-not populations and that of the developed world is narrowing. ... Economically free countries enjoy significantly greater prosperity than those burdened by heavy government intervention.'

Since capitalism has produced economic results that no other system has been able to duplicate, a normative issue could be raised: is it possible, and if so how, to move the community toward capitalism via voluntary interactions among freely-choosing individuals and with only limited involvement of the state?

THE RULE OF LAW AND BASIC FORMAL INSTITUTIONS OF CAPITALISM

Achieving the transformation of classical liberalism into capitalism required a set of formal institutions strong enough to secure individual liberties, enforce private property rights, create incentives to reduce the transaction costs of exchange and maintain competitive markets. Those institutions structure the rule of law. The rule of law, then, was a major vehicle for the institutionalization of classical liberalism into capitalism.

Bruno Leoni (1961, pp. 59–76) and Friedrich Hayek (1960, chs 11–12) argued that the rule of law has to satisfy three key elements: *the absence of arbitrary power* on the part of the ruling elite, which means that no laws are enacted with the intent of helping or harming particular individuals or groups; *equality before the law*, which guarantees that all citizens, including members of the ruling group, are subject to the same laws enforced by independent courts; and a well-defined procedure for replacing the ruling group, such as regularly scheduled *democratic elections*.[1] Friedrich Hayek (1955) pointed out that a major economic consequence of substituting the rule of law for the arbitrary state was a huge increase in the economic efficiency of resolving the issues of who gets what and who does what.

The purpose of the rule of law is to tame the discretionary power of government and thus enable individuals to pursue their private ends in an efficiency-friendly way, as argued in Chapter 1. On the other hand, the rule of men is about the power of the ruling group to make discretionary changes in the pursuit of its own ends. A major difference between the rule of law and the rule of men is that the rule of law requires a well-defined, stable and credible process by which formal rules can be changed. In a rule of men state, changes in formal rules are a vehicle through which the ruling group seeks its ends. Thus the rule of men deprives individuals of the credible right of ownership and the freedom of contract (Pipes, 1999, p. 25).

The rule of law is a scarce good. That is why it is not readily observed. Like all scarce goods, the rule of law needs to be produced and maintained. Production of new rules and the maintenance of existing is costly because it uses scarce resources.

The production of a new formal rule in civil code countries requires grants to universities and think-tanks to produce studies and generate expert testimony, and it calls for long debates in parliaments and the media about the merits and demerits of proposed rules. Major constraints on legislators' choice of new rules are the perceived views of the median voter and the support from rent-seeking coalitions. The process of making a new precedent in common law involves mostly court costs. Given the adversarial nature of court proceedings in the United States, a good percentage of those costs are 'privatized'; that is, they are borne by the parties involved. Major constraints on common law judges wishing to violate existing precedents are tradition and customs, and the review of their rulings by higher courts.

Many individual and organized groups have incentives to erode the institutions embodied by the rule of law. This means that the rule of law requires maintenance, and the maintenance of formal rules requires a well-defined procedure for their safeguarding. The procedure for making new rules has to be well-defined and also has to have a strong bias in favor of the status quo. Being entrenched in tradition and customs, common law formal rules (i.e., precedents) are more difficult to change than any formal rules in civil law countries, where legislators are subject to the current interpretation of social justice by the median voter.

Recognizing the importance of constraining changes in formal rules, Nobel laureate James Buchanan (1972, p. 452), wrote that his approach has 'an explicit prejudice in favor of previously existing rights, not because this structure possesses some intrinsic ethical attributes, and not because change in itself is undesirable, but for the much more elementary reason that only such prejudice offers incentives for the emergence of voluntary negotiated settlements among the parties themselves. Indirectly, therefore, this prejudice guarantees that resort to the state is effectively minimized.'

We can think of the rule of law, then, as the container holding a set of well-defined formal institutions that satisfy the conditions stipulated by Hayek and Leoni, are costly to produce, and generate benefits in excess of the costs of producing and maintaining them. Perusing academic literature of capitalism indicates that the most important formal institutions setting capitalism apart from other systems are private property rights, the law of contract, an independent judiciary and a constitution. While many other institutions are part of the system, the container we call the rule of law must include those four formal rules.

If private property rights, the law of contract, an independent judiciary and a constitution are major institutions in the container of the rule of law, their economic implications must be largely responsible for the observed performance of the free-market, private-property economy. And differences in the credibility and stability of those four institutions, on a country-by-country basis, should explain differences in economic performance.

The idealized concept of capitalism based on the rule of law and competitive markets probably never existed. However, its four basic institutions, which exemplify the rule of law, exist in all countries in the West. In some countries those institutions are more attenuated than in others, yet they do exist. Thus the rule of law and competitive markets are not merely ideal or imaginary concepts for protecting competition, freedom of exchange and individual liberty. By implication they are also a useful yardstick against which we can evaluate both the prevailing formal institutions of capitalism in different communities and the consistency of any proposed institutional reform with the private-property, free-market economy. The Index of Economic Freedom provides evidence on a country-by-country basis about the relationship between the attenuation of the rule of law and economic performance. This relationship is discussed in some detail in Chapter 8.

Analysis of capitalism based on the incentive effects of its four basic institutions is then a realistic point of departure for better understanding of the economic forces at work. One can argue that the four basic institutions of capitalism, however attenuated they might be, have been the source of energy that explains the economic performance of the West vs. the Rest. Moreover, non-Western countries that have accepted some features of the rule of law and/or open markets have been performing better than others.

The four institutions contained in the rule of law and open markets require that the government be strong enough to protect the rights of the governed. However, the necessity of transferring some decision-making powers from individuals to their respective governments opens a window of opportunity for legislators, judges and bureaucrats to expand the role of the state and, in doing so, to wipe out individual rights (Federalist Papers, no.10 and 51). An expansion of the role of the state in economic affairs raises the transaction costs of exchange, reduces the extent of voluntary exchange and consequently makes the economy less efficient.

The protection of individual rights and the taming of discretionary powers of the state are therefore associated with the term 'limited *government*'. The term refers more to the constraints on the number of government's functions than to its size. For example, England might have a large number of policemen and still be a limited government. Since more government means that more resources are withdrawn from the process of voluntary interactions in open markets, limiting the number of functions performed by the state enhances economic efficiency.

Private property rights, the law of contract, an independent judiciary and a constitution are the key building blocks of the private-property, free-market economy. They provide freely choosing individuals with strong incentives to minimize the transaction costs of voluntarily seeking the highest-valued uses for scarce resources and accepting the risk of innovating activity. The following three chapters discuss in some detail the economic implications of these basic institutions of capitalism.

THE SIGNIFICANCE OF CREDIBLE AND STABLE RULE OF LAW

Major economic functions of the rule of law are to protect competition and the freedom of exchange, and to minimize the discretionary power of the state. In order to perform those functions, the rule of law must be stable and credible. Otherwise the rule of law would resemble what G. Warren Nutter (1969, p. 39) once said about the former Soviet Union:

> It was Lenin's genius to recognize the importance of embellishing the Soviet system with all the trappings of democracy. If the people want a constitution, give them one, and even include the bill of rights. If they want a parliament, give them that, too. And a system of courts. If they want a federal system, create that myth as well. Above all, let them have elections, for the act of voting is what the common man most clearly associates with democracy. Give them all these, but make sure that they have no effect on how things are run.

The *credibility* of rules depends on their enforcement. A car-dealer's promise to take care of possible defects in the car is a valuable benefit to customers, provided that contracts are enforced. The enforcement of property rights in my home increases the flow of benefits from owning it. A professor's incentives to research a politically sensitive subject depend on the credibility of tenure.

The flow of benefits from the rule of law also depends on its *stability*. The purchase of land, investments in various assets, the choice of career, the choice of investment in children, and many other current decisions have long-run consequences. Frequent changes in the rules of the game, or expectations about frequent changes in the rules, increase the risk and uncertainty associated with activities that have future value consequences. A higher discount rate is a predictable consequence of changes in risk and uncertainty. And a higher discount rate means a bias in favor of exchanges with short-run consequences.

A few examples reveal the effect. The political position of Jews in medieval Europe was relatively insecure. Predictably, they favored investments in jewelry, gold coins and other liquid assets. South Americans prefer lower rates of return from investments in the United States to the much higher rates of return that are often available in their homelands. An investor in Putin's Russia faces a greater risk of expropriation than does an investor in, say, Slovenia; hence the payout period in Russia has to be shorter. Stable rules encourage individuals and organizations to seek the highest-valued uses for their goods regardless of time horizons.

The importance of stable and credible rules is traceable to ancient times. As Leoni (1961, p. 62) reminds us: 'Aristotle knew well the harm that an arbitrary and unpredictable rule could cause to ordinary people in his day ... and Cicero echoed this Aristotelian conception in his famous dictum ... we must all obey the law if we were to be free'. I have elsewhere (1998, p. 26) explained the importance of stable and credible institutions as follows:

> Comparison with a football game may illustrate the consequences of unstable institutions. In football, the rules of the game are set. Fans enjoy watching the game. Players know how to play it. And coaches know how to prepare their players. However, during an important game the blue team is on the one-yard line and fails to execute the fourth down. The coach goes to the referee and pleads: 'My players worked so hard to get to the goal line, please give them another down?' Suppose the referee has power to choose to go along with the request, and the blue team scores. In the short run the blue team has won. But frequent changes in the rules would raise the costs of the game downstream. Football fans would not be able to enjoy the game, players would not know how to prepare for it, and football clubs would seek coaches who are better at getting rules changed than at coaching the players.

INFORMAL INSTITUTIONS OF CAPITALISM OR THE CULTURE OF INDIVIDUALISM

The incentive effects of the basic institutions of capitalism require a culture that encourages behavior based on self-interest, self-responsibility and self-determination. However, such behavior does not occur in a moral vacuum. The culture of individualism has emerged and is entrenched in a set of informal rules that combine the Greek inquisitive reasoning, the Roman concept of law and the Christian-Judeo religious beliefs. Like the rule of law, the culture of individualism is also a Western phenomenon.[2]

In the sixth century, Pope Gregory I initiated the process that eventually replaced the extended family with the nuclear family. Gregory I did it by overturning four traditional and legal practices: marriage to close kin, marriage to the widows of close kin, the transfer of children by adoption, and concubinage (Lal, 1998, p. 83). The behavioral consequences of the nuclear family and the extended family on the development of the culture of capitalism can hardly be exaggerated. The rise of the nuclear family illustrates major differences between the culture of individualism and the culture of collectivism. By encouraging the concept of a polity consisting of natural equals, the nuclear family creates incentives for bonding among individuals across family lines. By emphasizing egalitarianism and collectivism, the extended family raises the transaction costs of interactions between individuals belonging to different groups.

Institutional reforms initiated in the eleventh century by Pope Gregory VII provided cultural unity as well as the enforcement of property rights and contracts in a politically decentralized Europe. The rise of individualism in thirteenth-century England has already been noted. The alienation of philosophy from theology in the fourteenth through sixteenth centuries initiated the revival of the inquisitive Greek spirit. The Reformation encouraged individualism and the work ethic. It also opened the market for salvation by offering an alternative to the Roman Church's interpretation of guidance to the attainment of redemption.

Alberto Alesina and George-Marios Angeletos (2002) noted some interesting cultural differences in the way Americans and Europeans react to income inequalities. While 71 percent of Americans maintain that the poor could pull themselves up by their bootstraps, only 40 percent of Europeans think so. Hence, we observe that the alleviation of poverty in the United States emphasizes work effort, while European governments prefer redistributive policies from above.

The culture of individualism has been changing in the West. Those changes have led to a weak resistance to the ever-increasing role of the state in the economy via the infusion of statutes and regulations into the legal system, and the result of this infusion of statutes and regulations has been the attenuation of capitalism in the West. Focusing on the relationship between individual liberty and credible private property rights versus the regulatory acts of the state, James Buchanan, a Nobel Laureate for Economics, explains changes in the culture of individualism in the article 'Afraid to Be Free: Dependency as Desideratum', which is reprinted below.

NOTES

1. It should be noted, however, that although Leoni and Hayek did share the same definition, they differed in approach and thus in the evaluation of the outcomes.
2. As a reminder, in this book the terms 'culture of individualism' and 'culture of capitalism' are used interchangeably.

REFERENCES

Alesina, A. and G. Angeletos (2002), 'Fairness and redistribution: US vs. Europe', *Working Paper*, No. 9502, National Bureau for Economic Research, New York.

Buchanan, J. (1972), 'Politics, property and the law: an alternative interpretation of Miller et al. v. Schoene,' *Journal of Law and Economics*, **15**(2), 439–52.

Federalist Papers (1998), Washington, DC: Library of Congress.

Hayek, F. (1955), 'The political ideal and the rule of law', in *Fiftieth Anniversary Commemoration Lectures,* Cairo: National Bank of Egypt.

Hayek, F. (1960), *The Constitution of Liberty*, Chicago: University of Chicago Press.

Lal, D. (1998), *Unintended Consequences*, Cambridge: MIT Press.

Leoni, B. (1961), *Freedom and the Law*, New York: Van Nostrand Company.

Macfarlane, Alan (1978), *The Origins of English Individualism*, London: Blackwell.

Nutter, W. (1969), *The Strange World of Ivan Ivanov*, New York: World Publishing Company.

O'Grady, M. (2007), 'The poor get richer', *Wall Street Journal*, 16 January.

Opp, K.D. (1983), 'Problems of defining and explaining capitalism', in S. Pejovich (ed.), *Philosophical and Economic Foundations of Capitalism*, New York: Lexington Press, pp. 25-31.

Pejovich, S. (1998), *Economic Analysis of Institutions and Systems*, Dordrecht: Kluwer Academic Publishers (revised 2nd edn).

Pipes, Richard (1999), *Property and Freedom*, New York: Alfred Knopf.

Schumpeter, J. (1954), *History of Economic Analysis*, Oxford: Oxford University Press.

Sombart, W. (1902), *Der Moderne Kapitalismus*, Berlin: Duncker & Humblot.

Appendix: Afraid to be free: dependency as desideratum

James M. Buchanan

I INTRODUCTION

For this special issue, the editors asked me specifically to submit an essay under the general title, 'Capitalism, Socialism, and Democracy in the Twenty-First Century'. In this solicitation, they were encouraging me to think in grandiose terms, to offer a public choice–constitutional political economy perspective on the larger organizational–ideological alternatives that may emerge. We do not, of course, either collectively or privately, make choices as among the grand organizational alternatives. For the most part, and most of the time, we make choices on the various margins that present themselves, with the result that all societies are more or less capitalistic, more or less socialistic, more or less democratic. Nonetheless, these Schumpeterian terms may be helpful in organizing my general argument.

This argument can be succinctly summarized. If we loosely describe socialism in terms of the range and scope of collectivized controls over individual liberty of actions, then 'socialism' will survive and be extended. This result will emerge not because collectivization is judged to be more efficient, in some meaningful economic sense, or even because collectivization more adequately meets agreed upon criteria for distributive justice, but rather because only under the aegis of collective control, under 'the state' can individuals escape, evade and even deny personal responsibilities. In short, persons are afraid to be free. As subsequent discussion will suggest, socialism, as a coherent ideology, has lost most of its appeal. But, in a broader and more comprehensive historical perspective, during the course of two centuries, the state has replaced God as the father–mother of last resort, and persons will demand that this protectorate role be satisfied and amplified.

'Capitalism', an unfortunate but widely used term, again loosely described in terms of the range and scope for individual liberty of action outside collectiv-

* Reprinted with kind permission from Springer Science and Business Media from *Public Choice Journal* (2005), **124**(2), 19–31.

ized direction and control, must remain vulnerable to continuing marginal encroachments, and this thrust of change will remain despite possible analytical and empirical evidence that such encroachments signal retrogression along widely recognized success indicators.

'Democracy', defined broadly enough to include its many institutional variants, will reflect the preferences of the citizenry, who remain largely immune from the findings of science, and the increasing corruption that must necessarily accompany any expanding range of collective-political control will simply be tolerated and ignored. An overarching theme of the whole essay is that the thrust of development will be dictated by 'bottom up' demands rather than by 'top down' dictates of an elite.

I shall flesh out this general argument in later sections. Only in the final section of the essay shall I offer a more hopeful alternative to the pessimistic scenario sketched out above. Such an alternative emerges, however, as much from a sense of moral obligation to believe that constructive reform is within the possible as it does from any realistic prognosis of elements which are discernible beneath the surface of that which may be now observed.

II   THE SOURCES OF SOCIALISM

There are at least four sources or wellsprings of ideas that motivate extensions in the range and scope of collective controls over the freedom of persons to act as they might independently choose. In the political dialogue these sources are, of course, intermingled, but in philosophical discourse it seems useful to make distinctions. I shall label these four sources as (1) managerial, (2) paternalistic, (3) distributionist, and (4) parental. I shall discuss the first three of these four categories in this section. I shall treat the fourth source, that of the parental motivation, separately in section III, because I suggest that this source has been relatively neglected by analysts and, more importantly, that it is likely to swamp the other three in influence during the early decades of this new century.

Managerial Socialism

This is the form of socialism that is now dead and buried, both in ideas and in practice, having been 'done in' during the last decades of the twentieth century. This is the socialism that is defined as the collective ownership and control of the means of production, and which involves efforts at centralized command and direction of a national economy as institutionalized through a central planning authority. It is now almost universally acknowledged that the motivating ideas here were based on scientific–intellectual errors of major proportions – errors summarized under Hayek's rubric of 'fatal conceit'. Even in its idealized form, the construction involved a ubiquity of perverse incentives and ignored the impossibility of ascertaining knowledge from widely dispersed and dynamic relationships. The scientific flaws now seem evident, but the cautionary lesson to be learned is that, for a whole century, among the best and the brightest among the economists and philosophers, indeed among the intelligentsia and academics generally, discussion was carried on in what now seems a setting of amazing ignorance.

And with tragic consequences. Efforts to implement the idealized and basically flawed construction, whether piecemeal or in total, ran up against the limits imposed by the necessity that ordinary mortals rather than idealized automatons must operate the system. The gross inefficiency that should have been minimally predicted emerged; corruption itself became the only lubricant for otherwise rigid structures of interaction; rewards disproportionately favored opportunistic behavior; personalized favoritism was matched by unalloyed cruelty in the absence of effective exit options.

The economy allegedly organized on the command-control principles of managerial socialism simply cannot, and demonstrably could not, deliver the goods in any manner even remotely comparable to those economies organized under the principles derivative from Adam Smith's system of natural liberty. This variant of socialism, which found much of its origin in the highly successful Marxist ideological thrust, will not soon resurface. The first half of this new century will not witness demands for collectivized planning for planning's sake.

Paternalistic Socialism

The demise of managerial socialism has not, however, substantially lessened the demands for collectivization that stem from the alternative sources, including recognition by self-anointed elites that only by collectivization can the choices and actions of the masses be directed toward those patterns that 'should be wanted if these masses only knew what was in their own best interest'. This attitude, or set of attitudes, was importantly present in the imposition of managerial socialism, but, conceptually at least, it can be separately examined and analyzed. The ultimate motivation here need not stem from any argument to the effect that collective control is, in any sense, more 'efficient', as defined in some neutral aggregative value dimension. The motivation is located in the value scalar itself; that which persons privately express is not that which the elite prefer. Preferences need to be shifted in more acceptable directions. The French term, *dirigisme*, is actually more descriptive of this mind-set than any comparable English term.

The persons who adopt this stance do not necessarily object to capitalism, or, rather, the market process, as the allocative means of implementing their objectives. Indeed, the market may be left to do the heavy lifting, so long as the incentives are collectively adjusted so as to guarantee results dictated by the normative ideals of the elite. Much of the current political dialogue is imbued with this set of attitudes, notably much of the environmental emphasis, along with the impassioned crusades against tobacco and obesity.

This source of support for a widened collective control over liberty of choice will not fade away. It seems unlikely, however, that it will come to exert a major force toward further socialization. The limits of such efforts are exemplified, historically, by the failed experiment with prohibition of alcohol in the United States in the first third of the twentieth century and by Hillary Clinton's aborted effort in the early 1990s to remake the medical care industry. In this case, 'democracy', howsoever its complex processes may actually work, becomes a conservative bastion against efforts by any elite to impose its own value structure through collectivized coercion.

Distributionist Socialism

'Socialism is about equality' – this short statement moved quickly onto the center stage of discussion after the apparent demise of central planning and control. The advocates of centrally managed economies moved with surprising alacrity to align themselves with the welfare state, social democrats. The gross scientific errors that had produced the fatal conceit were swept aside as if they had never been promulgated, with the argument that, all along, distributional equality is and had remained the primary value for socialists of all stripes. Nor is the distributionist thrust absent from the arguments of the paternalists, whose attention may be focused on in-kind transfers of defined goods and services to designated recipients, but always aimed in the direction of more equality in the final access to such goods.

In its unadulterated form, however, the distributionist argument is exclusively about equality, or rather inequality, in the distribution of goods and services, without concern for the make-up of the bundle. The allocative function may be left exclusively to the market (capitalism), as it responds to the preference patterns of persons as consumers and producers within the post-tax, post-transfer redistributional limits. The focus here is not upon what the market generates, or even on how it operates, but rather on the distributional outcomes that would emerge in the absence of the specifically directed and collectivized tax-transfer structure.

At the level of abstract political philosophy, and notably as brought into modern attention through the work of John Rawls, this source for collective action is the only one that is at all consistent with the precepts of classical liberalism. Even the hard-core libertarians find it difficult to defend the unconstrained distributional outcomes of the market process, of unrestricted capitalism, as embodying widely shared norms for fairness. Even when the perverse incentives that arise on both the tax and transfer sides of the fiscal account are fully recognized, and even if the shortfalls between the stylized distributional adjustments that may be imagined and the actual adjustments that are possible through democratic politics are also taken into account, widespread support for some distributional correction may be evidenced. And, to the extent that the socialized sector of activity is measured so as to include the tax-transfer budget, 'socialism' seems unlikely to disappear from observed political reality.

Support for extending this tax-transfer budget, as motivated by strictly redistributionist objectives, may, however, be much less than implied by the oft-encountered class warfare demagoguery of electoral politics. The poor, the distributionally disadvantaged, are not observed to be using the majoritarian processes of democracy to exploit the rich, at least beyond relatively narrow limits. And, indeed, much of the class warfare rhetoric seems to reflect the ranting of the elitists who call on the distributionist motivation to advance their basic *dirigisme*.

III   PARENTAL SOCIALISM

To my knowledge, the term 'parental' has never been explicitly discussed as being descriptive of the motivation behind the collectivization–socialization of human activity. I introduce this term here for want of a better one to describe a source that is difficult to encapsulate even if easy to treat in more extended discussion. In one sense, the attitude is paternalism flipped over, so to speak. With paternalism, we refer to the attitudes of elitists who seek to impose their own preferred values on others. With *parentalism*, in contrast, we refer to the attitudes of persons who seek *to have values imposed upon them* by other persons, by the state, or by transcendental forces. This source of support for expanded collectivization has been relatively neglected by both socialist and liberal philosophers, perhaps because the philosophers, in both camps, remain methodological individualists.

As the title for this essay indicates, and as I have noted earlier, this ultimate motivation for maintenance and extension of control over the activities of persons through collective institutions will, in my assessment, be more important in shaping the patterns of development during the first half of the new century than any of the other, and more familiar, sources discussed in the previous section. Almost subconsciously, those scientists–scholars–academicians who have tried to look at the 'big picture' have assumed that, other things being equal, persons want to be at liberty to make their own choices, to be free from coercion by others, including indirect coercion through means of persuasion. They have failed to emphasize sufficiently, and to examine the implications of, the fact that liberty carries with it *responsibility*. And it seems evident that many persons do not want to shoulder the final responsibility for their own actions. Many persons are, indeed, afraid to be free.

The term 'parental' becomes quite descriptive in its inference that the attitude here is akin to that of the child who seeks the cocoon-like protection of its parents, and who may enjoy its liberty but only within the limits defined by the range of such protection. The mother or father will catch the child if it falls, will bandage its cuts, will excuse its behavioral excesses along all dimensions. Knowledge that these things will be done provides the child with a sense of order in its universe, with elements of predictability in uncertain aspects of the environment.

This cozy setting is dramatically disturbed when the child becomes an adult, when responsibility must be shouldered independently from the family bounds. Relatively few persons are sufficiently strong, as individuals, to take on the full range of liberties and their accompanying responsibilities without seeking some substitute or replacement of the parental shelter. Religion, or God as the transcendent force that exemplifies fatherhood or motherhood, has and does serve this purpose (more on this below). Organized community is a less satisfactory but nonetheless partial parental replacement for some persons. More importantly, and specifically for purposes of the discussion here, the collectivity – the state – steps in and relieves the individual of his responsibility as an independently choosing and acting adult. In exchange, of course, the state reduces the liberty of the individual to act as he might choose. But the order that the state, as parent, provides may be, for many persons, well worth the sacrifice in liberty.

Note that, as mentioned earlier, the source for extension in collective or state control here is 'bottom up' rather than 'top down', as with paternalism. Persons who are afraid to take on independent responsibility that necessarily goes with liberty demand that the state fill the parental role in their lives. They *want* to be told what to do and when to do it; they seek order rather than uncertainty, and order comes at an opportunity cost they seem willing to bear.

The thirst or desire for freedom, and responsibility, is perhaps not nearly so universal as so many post-Enlightenment philosophers have assumed. What share of persons in varying degrees of bondage, from slavery to ordinary wage-salary contracts, really want to be free, with the accompanying responsibility for their own choices? The disastrous failure of 'forty acres and a mule' was followed by the lapse into renewed dependency status for emancipated former slaves in the American south. And the surprising strength of Communist parties in the politics of post-Cold War central and eastern Europe attests to the thirst on the part of many persons 'to be controlled'.

IV   GOD IS DEAD; LONG LIVE THE STATE

Prior to the eighteenth century, to the Enlightenment, and particularly in the West, God, as institutionally embodied in the church (and churches), fulfilled what seemed to be a natural role as the overarching 'parent', who assumed ultimate responsibility for the individual in a last-resort sense, as biological linkages were necessarily lost in the aging profile. Manifestations abound. 'We Are All God's Children', 'God Will Take Care of You' – these familiar hymnal assertions are merely illustrative of the near-universal attitude. Psychologically, persons went about their ordinary lives secure in the feeling that God would clear up any mess they might make, analogously to parents' behavior toward children. Of course, transgressions might be followed by punishment, in this or another life, but predictability characterized both the rules themselves and the prospect for both reward and punishment. God, as institutionally embodied, provided order in the lives of all.

But what if Nietzsche is right? What if God is dead? What happens to the person who is forced to recognize that the ordering presence of God is no longer real? What if God cannot be depended on to clean up the mess, even in some last resort sense? Who and/or what can fulfill the surrogate parent role? Who and what is there beyond the individual that can meet the yearning for family-like protectiveness? Who and what will pick us up when and if we fall? Who and what can provide the predictability that God and his agency structures seemed to offer?

In the more extensive idealizations, as imagined by some medieval scholastics, secular politics, or the state, is an unnecessary appendage to God's embodiment in the church. Nascent efforts in post-medieval centuries to establish secular authority independent of church control were opposed throughout the European realm, but the monopoly of the Catholic church was broken, by Luther and his followers, well before the onset of the Enlightenment. God was no longer monolithic in the image of one institution. Competing interpretations emerged, and the conflicts among churches came to be intermingled with conflicts among states as representatives of those churches. In the process, secular authority came to be divorced from ecclesiastical authority and to assume independent stature.

By the time of the Enlightenment, the secular nation-state had almost reached its maturity, and nationalism, the sense of nationhood, was a more or less natural repository for the sentiments of those persons for whom God had died. For many, the state, as the collectivity, moved into the gap left by the demise of the church's parental role. The individual who sought family-like protection, but who no longer sensed the presence of such protection in the church, or in God so embodied, found a substitute in the collectivity. The individual could feel that he or she 'belonged' to the larger community and was necessarily dependent on that community. The death of God and the birth of the national state, and especially in its latter-day welfare state form, are the two sides of the coin of history in this respect.

The transposition through which the state replaced God in the parental role, for many persons, was aided and abetted by two historically parallel developments. First, the Enlightenment, in itself, did not contain justification for the burgeoning of the state, as such. From the Enlightenment, classical liberalism rather than collectivism emerged. But, as the next section will indicate, classical liberalism singularly failed to offer persons any psychological security coincident with the loss of religious faith. Almost immediately following the Enlightenment, however, arguments for socialism, as treated above, were advanced. And all arguments for socialist organization depend critically on the expansion of the collectivized or politicized sector of activities.

Implementation of the socialist proposals for change, in whole or in part, was accomplished through the combination of Marxist ideology, paternalism of the intelligentsia, distributionist argument, and the residually desperate search for a parental replacement for God. Socialist collectivism promised the order that seemed absent in post-Enlightenment liberalism. Persons more or less readily accepted the dependency status that socialism carried with it because, by becoming dependants of the collectivity, they were able, at the same time, to share in the communal project that collectivism seemed to represent.

The state did, indeed, become God. This transposition was, of course, most evident in the Soviet Union and other Communist regimes, but essentially the same psychological shift in public attitudes took place in Western democratic societies. Persons accepted the dependence on the state as normal; even those who at the same time railed against the increasing collective–governmental intrusiveness. It came to be increasingly rare to find persons and groups who supported releasing the shackles of dependency. The collapse of the Communist regimes in the last decades of the century did little or nothing toward slowing down the growth of the welfare state; this, in itself, demonstrates that the parental motivation for collectivization remains perhaps the strongest of those identified above.

V   THE LACUNA OF CLASSICAL LIBERALISM

The central organizing idea of classical liberalism emerged from the Enlightenment, notably from its Scottish variants. This idea, best enunciated by Adam Smith, is that extensive collective direction and control over activity is not required at all, that, with minimally invasive institutions that guarantee person, property and contract, persons can be left at liberty to make their own choices and, in so doing, generate maximal value. The spontaneous order of the market, emergent as persons are allowed to make their own choices in a 'simple system of natural liberty', implies that there is only a limited role for the sovereign state.

Modern socialism, at least in the first three variants noted above, was born as a reaction against classical liberalism, and especially against the limited successes of classical political economy during the first half of the nineteenth century. As indicated, managerial or command-control socialism was based on intellectual error, on a failure to understand the basic principles of market order. Paternalistic socialism rejects the democratic features of market outcomes and, by inference, also rejects small-'d' democracy in governance. Distributional socialism can, as noted, be accommodated within classical liberalism by appropriate adjustments imposed on market outcomes.

The lacuna in classical liberalism lies in its failure to offer a satisfactory alternative to the socialist–collectivist thrust that reflects the pervasive desire for the parental role of the state. For persons who seek, even if unconsciously, dependence on the collectivity, the classical liberal argument for independence amounts to negation. Classical liberals have not involved themselves in the psychological elements of public support for or against the market order.

'The spontaneous order of the market' – this is an intellectual idea that is not naturally understood by those who have not been exposed to the teachings of economists. And economists themselves in their sometimes zeal for working out the intricacies of complex models have neglected their primary didactic purpose. They have assumed that, like the ideas in the natural sciences, once an idea is accepted by the scientific community it will become a part of the conventional wisdom of the public, as implemented in institutional reforms. Economists, as the putative repositories of the principles of classical liberalism, have not sensed the categorical differences in public reception of their scientific findings and those of their fellow natural scientists. In a very real sense, every person is his or her own economist, who pays little or no respect to the truths of economic science.

For far too many members of the body politic, the market order requires that persons subject themselves to 'the blind forces of the market', as if the independence so offered carries no offsetting gains. There is a widespread failure to understand that the independence offered by the entry and exit options of the market offsets the *dependence* on others when markets are closed or displaced. And such dependence, importantly, includes dependence on the state, and on its bureaucratic agents. The individual can readily walk away from a market relationship. He cannot walk away from the taxing authority.

The entry and exit options provided by the market serve as the omnipresent frontier open to all participants, and economists could well have done more to exploit the familiar frontier experience by instancing the analogue here. Their failure to do so illustrates the point made above, that adherents of classical liberalism, and especially economists, have not been sufficiently concerned with preaching the gospel of independence. Classical liberalism, properly understood, demonstrates that persons can stand alone, that they need neither God nor the state to serve as surrogate parents. But this lesson has not been learned.

VI   CAPITALISM AND ITS CONTRADICTIONS

Capitalism ('free enterprise' would be a much better term here) is the institutionalized embodiment of classical liberalism. As idealized, it is best described as a system in which values are set; resources are allocated; goods and services are produced and distributed through a network of voluntary exchanges among freely choosing–acting persons and groups – a network that functions within a collectively-imposed legal structure that protects persons and property and enforces contracts while at the same time financing those goods and services that are most efficiently shared among many users. Such an idealized capitalistic system would, at most, command collectively up to fifteen percent of national value product.

During the half-century since the Second World War, we have observed that, even in Western countries outside the nominally socialized Communist bloc, the collectivized sector has extended its allocative–distributive reach to estimates ranging from forty percent to sixty percent of total value generated. What are such systems to be called? Half capitalist and half socialist?

Contradictions become apparent once we recognize that the principles upon which the whole organizational structure allegedly rests are those derived from classical liberalism rather than from socialism in any form. It is as if these principles carry the politicized or socialist half of value on their backs, as it were, as a deadweight burden. Such principles include the rule of law, which requires that all persons, regardless of dependency status, be subjected to the same law, including, importantly, those who become agents for the collectivity. In addition, democracy, as a political form, requires open and universal franchise, with eligibility for agency roles being open to all. Within the appropriately defined jurisdiction, all persons are guaranteed freedom of entry and exit to and from occupational and geographical opportunities, subject only to the respect dictated by the legal protections noted above. All persons in the organized polity are insured that personal rights are protected – rights to speak, to practice religion, to associate with whom they may choose.

The listing might be extended, but the point made should be clear. There is no discrimination among persons in the implementation of the basic principles of classical liberalism. The implication is clear. To the extent that the burgeoning tax-transfer element in the budgets of modern democracies is motivated by demands that the state take on a parental role, this element must be characterized by *generality*. Persons become subject to tax on the one hand and eligible for transfer payments on the other by their membership in the polity and not by their identification as a member of this or that group, as defined in nongeneral terms (see Buchanan and Congleton, 1998). Any departure from the generality norm, any discrimination, must introduce classification among persons, which violates the classical liberal presupposition of equality.

Major programs in the welfare-state budgets are, at least nominally, organized on generality principles. Tax financed or pay-as-we-go pension schemes are general in coverage, although with built-in redistributive elements. Tax-financed medical services are open to all members of the community, although here, too, there are built-in redistributive features. Contradictions emerge, however, as the fiscal demands placed on these programs increase, almost explosively, in the fact of changing age profiles and rapid advances in medical technology. Pressures will increase, and indeed are already observed, to contain such demands in part by explicitly introducing departures from generality, by imposing means tests as criteria for eligibility for transfers. To the extent that changes are made in this direction, public support for the programs that stem from the parental motivation must decline. As increasing numbers of persons come to recognize that, with the changes, the state will no longer take care of them, even in some remote residual sense, their image of these programs is dramatically modified. The transfers will come to be viewed as discriminatory payments to politically selected groups, rather than transfers to an inclusive class of eligibles.

On the other hand, if the generality principle is preserved, even if not fully honored, the predictable demands on the fiscal capacities of the welfare states are simply not sustainable. Efforts to meet the commitments under the various programs, most notably the pension and medical services systems, would require that the extraction of taxes from pretax market returns go well beyond the limits that are behaviorally feasible, quite apart from public choice questions about political will. After all, the Laffer curve relationship is a very real constraint in any polity.

Almost without exception, the welfare-state democracies are being, and will be increasingly, confronted with the disjuncture in the two-pronged decision structure, which, ultimately, reflects the clash between classical liberalism and socialism. As their preferences are expressed through the political process, citizens may genuinely want to extend the parental role of the welfare state, to allow the state to replace God. At the same time, however, citizens may, at their private choice margins, seek to minimize their tax obligations. The liberal principle that persons are to be free to create taxable capacity as and if they so choose is not consistent with the socialist principle that the welfare dependency be expanded beyond plausibly acceptable fiscal limits. The first half of the new century will determine how this basic conflict may be resolved.

VII PREDICTION AND PROSPECT

Straightforward prediction, based on an assessment of the workings of democratic processes, as observed, would suggest that the budgetary pressures will provoke increasing departures from generality norms in various welfare programs. Means testing or targeting will be extended well beyond current levels. The ranks of those who are explicitly classified as dependants of the nanny state will be reduced, perhaps substantially. As noted, such a breakdown in the generality norm will be accompanied by withdrawal of political support as claimant groups come to be seen as net parasites on those who create taxable capacity. Western welfare democracies may well approach the model for 'the churning state', described by Anthony de Jasay, in which differing groups compete among themselves for claims against each other.

Of course, such predictions need not be fulfilled. As an example, consider predictions that might have been made, say, from the early 1970s. Who might have predicted that Margaret Thatcher's reforms would move Britain dramatically up in the European league tables; that Ronald Reagan would restore the American spirit; that the Soviet Union would collapse? Western welfare democracies have not yet passed the point of no return. Public attitudes, as reflected through political leaders, may come to embody the recognition that the collectively generated demands on the fisc cannot be met from revenues produced from tax structures that remain plausibly acceptable. The principle of generality in welfare programs may be maintained, more or less, as the demands are scaled back within reasonable limits. As such reforms are implemented, increasing numbers of the citizenry may actually slough off, at least in part, the sense of dependency on the state.

The legacy of Marx is a spent force. The legacy of Bismarck is alive and well. It can, however, be contained with leadership and understanding, as Bismarck himself thought possible.

POSTSCRIPT

This essay has been written on the presumption that terrorism, through the damage inflicted, the reaction and response, along with preventive measures, will not permanently change the basic institutions of Western democracies. If this presumption is invalid, the effects can only be to reinforce the central argument advanced. Terror, in actuality or in threat, almost necessarily places the individual citizen in a more enveloping dependency relation with the state. Events may dictate that the range and scope of collectivized controls be extended. And, along this dimension, even the ardent classical liberal finds difficulty in mounting effective opposition.

In such extension, a comparable tension to that instanced above will arise. Pressures will emerge for departures from the institutions of generality and toward the introduction of discrimination, with consequences that are perhaps worse than those involved under the welfare umbrella, narrowly defined.

REFERENCES

Buchanan, James M. and Roger D. Congleton (1998), *Politics by Priniciple, Not Interest: Toward Nondiscriminatory Democracy*, New York and Cambridge: Cambridge University Press.
Hayek, F.A. (1988), *The Fatal Conceit: The Errors of Socialism*, Chicago: University of Chicago Press.
de Jasay, Anthony (1985), *The State*, Oxford: Basil Blackwell.
Rawls, John (1971), *A Theory of Justice*, Cambridge, MA: Harvard University Press.

5. The law of contract and the judiciary

Chapter 1 addressed the costs and benefits of free exchange, which are the same as the costs and benefits of contracts and need not be repeated here. Individuals seek exchange because they expect that trade will make them better off. An unintended consequence of exchange is then to move goods from lower to higher valued uses. Chapter 2 explained that different institutions have different effects on transaction costs, and that changes in transaction costs, in turn, have different effects on the extent of exchange and on economic performance.

Avner Greif provided an excellent comparison of the efficiency of exchange under two different institutional arrangements in the eleventh to thirteenth centuries: the collectivist culture of the Maghribi community and the individualistic culture in Genoa. He found that the rules of the game in the Maghribi community created behavioral incentives characteristic of those that are common in the communities based on the extended family. Those are still observed in many underdeveloped countries. Genoa, in the pursuit of more trade, reduced the transaction costs of exchange by substituting formal (legal) contracts for informal sanctions. The enforcement of those contracts reduced the transaction costs of exchange across family lines and ethnic groups. Greif (1994, p. 942) summarized the implications of those differences as follows: 'Collectivist cultural beliefs led to a societal organization based on the group's ability to use economic, social, and, most likely, moral sanctions against deviants. In contrast, individualist cultural beliefs weakened the dependence of each individual on any specific group [and] led to a societal organization based on legal, political, and economic organizations for enforcement and coordination.'

Let us move Greif's analysis forward a few centuries. By freeing individuals from the constraints of the extended family, the culture of capitalism provided incentives for them to seek the most profitable exchanges regardless of whether those exchanges were found within or across family lines. However, incentives alone cannot overcome the high transaction costs of exchange with individuals we do not know or whose customs we do not understand. And neither can internal sanctions, which work well within the extended family but not across family lines. The law of contract, one of the basic institutions of capitalism, reduces the transaction costs of identifying, negotiating and enforcing exchange. In doing so, the law of contract enhances the economic efficiency of the private-property, free-market economy. Why?

By holding people to their promises, the law of contract (1) encourages exchanges that are not simultaneous, (2) reduces the transaction costs of moving durable goods to higher-valued uses, (3) prevents opportunistic behavior, and (4) alleviates unforeseen contingencies. Let us briefly explain each of those economic functions of the law of contract.

A offers to pay $5000 for my car now (i.e., upon getting possession), while B promises $6000 a year later (although the car is delivered now). If the rate of interest were less than 20 percent, I would prefer to sell my car to B. But I would sell my car to A *unless* the law of contract protects me. That is, by holding people to their promises, the law of contract removes the bias against non-simultaneous exchanges and encourages resources to move to their higher-valued uses.

Some exchanges, such as buying a car, getting married, purchasing a home, or acquiring a new computer, have consequences that extend well into the future. Thus some problems – most of them honest mistakes – are bound to emerge. In the case of many durable goods, the transaction costs of identifying problems are reduced as the goods are used. In those cases, the buyer is a lower-cost provider of information about the attributes of cars, homes and computers. By including warranties, guarantees and return privileges within the exchange package, the seller shifts the burden of discovering 'defects' to a lower-cost producer of such information, reduces the transaction costs of exchange and increases the volume of trade.

The law of contract also reduces the transaction costs of opportunistic behavior. As reported by Richard Posner (2003, p. 100), in *Alaska Packers' Association* v. *Domenico*, the owner of a boat hired a group of workers to fish for him off the coast of Alaska. The wages were agreed to before the trip began. When the ship arrived in Alaskan waters, the workers asked for higher wages. Having no way of replacing them, the owner agreed. However, upon return to San Francisco, he paid his workers only the initially agreed wages. The workers sued him and lost. The court held that the defendant's promise to pay the wages over and above the original contract was not supported by fresh consideration (reciprocal promise). The decision was efficiency-friendly because it reduced incentives for opportunistic behavior in the future.

The transaction costs of drawing up detailed contracts that include all foreseeable problems are high. Moreover, some problems cannot be foreseen. In most modern legal systems, the law of contract covers contingencies that the parties to exchange did not consider. The question a judge has to decide is what the parties would have done had they been able to predict the event that brought them to court, and the judge then applies the customary rule. Posner (2003, p. 97) gives the following example: 'A buys goods from B, with delivery to take place in a month, and during the month B's warehouse burns down and the goods are destroyed. The contract is silent on the allocation of the risk of loss before delivery. But since B can prevent (or insure against) a fire in his own warehouse at lower cost than A can, the parties, if they had thought about the matter, would probably have assigned the risk to B.'

Finally, consider a case where a breach of contract involves the loss of reputation. In a competitive economy reputation is a source of wealth. It takes time and resources to earn a good reputation. A reputable car dealer can charge more for cars than a fly-by-night salesman. The difference in price is the return on the investment in a reputation for honest dealing.

Reputation is also costly to maintain. Breach of a contract might yield larger profits now but at the cost of losing customers down the road. It can also work the other way around. Suppose that merchant A expects to be in business 20 years, while merchant B plans to quit business in two years after 15 years of good services to customers. Also suppose that the immediate gains from going back on contractual promises to their customers are the same for both merchants. However, the costs are not the same, because the two have different time horizons. If merchant A went back on a contract, the present value of future losses from a declining reputation is likely to be greater than the immediate pecuniary gains. On the other hand, if merchant B went back on a contract, the present value of future losses could easily be less than the immediate pecuniary gains. However, when the legal system enforces contracts, A and B would find cheating equally expensive.

INDEPENDENT JUDICIARY

An independent judiciary means that judges expect their decisions to be carried out and that they are free (in terms of income and career) from backlash by legislators and bureaucrats. The term 'independent judiciary' says nothing about the character and/or ability of judges. There will always be good and bad judges as well as honest and not-so-honest judges. An inquiry into how well an independent judiciary serves the rule of law raises the issues of the accountability of judges and the power of independent judiciary to protect the legal and economic system from the other two branches of government and from international organizations.

The Accountability of Judges

Lack of judicial independence is a characteristic of the rule of men and is therefore not discussed here. We can note in passing that judicial dependence does not rule out the accountability of judges. Soviet judges were fully dependent on the state, yet their accountability was extraordinary by any measure: they were quite diligent in applying the rules that the Central Committee of the Communist Party supplied daily.

Any lack of accountability by judges has a cost, which is some attenuation of the rule of law. It is important, then, that the system restrain judges from not being accountable. The analysis has then to identify the factors upon which the accountability of judges depends and the circumstances affecting those factors. In common law countries, two major factors that constrain judges are the obligation to justify their decisions by reference to precedents and the apprehension of being reversed by a higher court. In civil law countries, two major factors that define the accountability of judges are the obligation to base their judgments on laws enacted by legislators and the apprehension of being reversed by a higher court. A major circumstance upon which those factors depend in both legal systems is the transaction costs of monitoring judges' rulings.

An implication is that the transaction costs of monitoring judges are positive. Otherwise, the accountability of judges would not have been an issue. Positive transaction costs, in turn, create discretionary power for judges to use personal preferences in interpreting the law. Since using personal preferences in deciding cases attenuates the rule of law, the accountability of judges in different countries should correlate with scores in the Index of Economic Freedom published jointly by the Heritage Foundation and the *Wall Street Journal*.

The Index of Economic Freedom compares, in effect, the strength of the rule of law in a wide range of countries. In this index, a score of 1 represents the non-attenuated rule of law. Scores above 1 represent various degrees of attenuation of the rule of law. By implication, the accountability of judges could be a contributing factor.

For example, scores for Italy and Germany (on a scale of 1 to 5, with 1 being the best) in the 2006 Index were 2.50 and 1.96, respectively. Not surprisingly, scores for the Italian and German judiciaries in Fraser's annual report of *Economic Freedom of the World* for 2004, which ranks independent judiciaries as one of its subcategories, were 4.2 and 8.8, respectively (Fraser's scores are on a scale of 1 to 10, with 10 being the best). Enrico Colombatto argues that the Italian judiciary is proud of its independence, to the point that many judges feel no restraint in interpreting the law against commonly established standards, or in taking sides following their political inclinations, or in going on strike in order to oppose legislation against their own interests (e.g., salary cuts).

The Power of an Independent Judiciary Relative to other Branches of Government

In the United States the president's power to veto legislative acts of the US Congress and the process of 'judicial review' are two key mechanisms for keeping ordinary laws and regulations in tune with the Constitution. While the president may veto legislative acts of Congress for purely political reasons (and Congress needs a two-third majority to override the president's veto), the judicial review of laws and regulations questions their conformity with the Constitution. According to Meese and colleagues (2005, p. 5), judicial review is, 'in a fundamental way, unique [to the US Constitution], for the Court is charged routinely, day in and day out, with the awesome task of addressing some of the most basic and most enduring political questions'. Within the area of its jurisdiction, a federal court in the United States can set aside a law enacted by Congress as unconstitutional. A major constraint on federal judges in setting aside laws enacted by Congress or regulations issued by the executive branch of the government is that they have to explain their rulings (which are often widely publicized) by reference to the Constitution.

In the Swiss Constitution federal laws are not subject to judicial review but can be challenged by a majority (Moser, 1994). However all cantonal laws become subject to judicial review if citizens require it. In Italy, laws can be sent back to Parliament by the president of the republic. But the president can raise no further objection if the law is voted into effect again. In Germany, the law for which constitutionality is being questioned is enforced until the Constitutional Court makes the final ruling. And those procedures take a long time in all countries. Thus judicial review is more effective in the United States, where the law is set aside until a higher court makes its ruling.

Court proceedings are also different in common law and civil law countries. Civil law countries use the inquisitorial system. In that system, judges take the leading role in gathering evidence and framing the issues, while the attorneys play a subordinate role. The inquisitorial process requires many more judges and fewer attorneys than the adversarial process. While the total costs of the inquisitional system might be lower, the adversarial system, which comes close to privatizing court proceedings, gives the parties in civil suits the freedom to determine the cost they are willing to accept relative to the expected benefits of winning the case.

The adversarial system used in common law countries requires that all the work be done by attorneys representing the plaintiff and the defendant. They investigate the circumstances of the case before the court; search for, collect and organize evidence; interrogate witnesses, check for the accuracy of information, and argue for the admissibility of evidence. Those costs, including attorneys' fees, are borne by the litigants themselves. In that sense, the adversarial system almost privatizes court proceedings. The qualification 'almost' applies because many costs (e.g., judge's salary, court personnel, equipment, etc) are borne by the state. The rationale is that the cases decided now benefit future litigants.

The common law judge is a relatively passive agent whose role is limited to monitoring the legality of procedure, making sure that the rules of evidence are observed and resolving various procedural issues that arise during trial. For example, the U.S. Supreme Court ruled that the State of California violated a defendant's Sixth Amendment right to a fair trial because a jury, not the judge, should decide details that can lengthen a sentence (*Cunningham* v *California,* 200, No. 05-6551).

In a very interesting research study, Elizabeth Brubaker argued that common law judges focus on using the past to 'discover' law for cases at hand, and in so doing they focus on the rights of individuals at the expense of the 'public interest'. Here are three cases from three different common law countries, as reported in Brubaker's study (1998).

In 1851, the City of Birmingham built a large sewer that polluted the Tame River. The owner of a downstream property complained that the pollution was killing fish, and affecting the health of his cows and sheep. He asked the court to issue an injunction. The City admitted that the sewer was polluting the river. However, it invoked the public good argument. It said that the 250 000 inhabitants of Birmingham would suffer from a plague or some other dreadful disease unless the sewer was allowed. In dismissing the City's argument, the judge said that he was not a public safety committee and that his function was to interpret the law, which in this case meant to protect the right of a property owner to enjoy a clean river.

In 1900, a paper mill in Indiana polluted a creek. Damages to the owner of property downstream were estimated at about $250. The paper mill's investment in the plant was about $90 000. The mill also employed a number of local people. In issuing an injunction against the mill, the judge was not moved by the numbers. He ruled that the mill violated private property rights and that the size of company investment was irrelevant.

In 1984, the High Court of Ontario, Canada, said that the defense of the general benefit of the community was not applicable in answer to a claim for nuisance. Five years later, the Canadian Supreme Court confirmed the court's reluctance to override common law property rights.

By protecting private property from intrusions by legislators and/or bureaucrats hiding their preferences behind a façade of words about social welfare or the public interest, common law judges made it possible for the parties directly interested in acquiring those rights to negotiate contracts (i.e., follow the Coase theorem) that would move resources to higher-valued uses. That is so because, once property rights are clearly defined, they could be transferred from lower- to higher-value users (e.g., the story in Chapter 2).

The International Court of Justice and an Independent Judiciary

The proliferation of statutes and government regulations since the 1930s has been breaking down the close relationship that existed in the United States between informal institutions and common law precedents However, yet another threat of alienating the country's legal system from its traditions and customs is gathering strength. Foreign governments as well as non-government organizations in the United States have been pressing the United States government to accept the resolutions and decisions made by international organizations such as the United Nations, and to recognize the International Court of Justice as a 'super supreme court'.

The United States has never refused to participate in the work of international organizations, but the United States does not consider the resolutions made by international organizations to be binding. Instead, the US government sees international organizations as an international market for discussion of issues between different states. In terms of economics, the function of international organizations is to reduce the transaction costs of resolving conflicts of interest between various states and regions. The final decision concerning the acceptance of the recommendations of international bodies should, however, remain in the hands of sovereign states. To accept the resolutions passed by international organizations would be to violate the US Constitution. The Kyoto Treaty is a good example. President George W. Bush has been widely criticized for not submitting the United States to the terms of this treaty. Yet foreign treaties have to be approved by the US Senate, and informal polling by President Clinton in the late 1990s showed that more than 90 senators (out of 100) would vote against approval of the Kyoto Treaty.

United States participation in international courts, specifically the International Court of Justice (ICJ), is an even more complicated issue, which domestic and foreign critics have overlooked at best or intentionally ignored at worst. Within the United States, support for accepting the ICJ as a super supreme court comes primarily from diplomats who expect more power for themselves, academics who hope for more grants for research, attorneys who expect more work and more money, and various environmental groups who hope that foreign judges may be more willing than the elected representative to impose environmental restrictions on the United States.

The problems with making IJC into a super supreme court are many. It is difficult to envision that ICJ judges from legal traditions as different as those of France and Portugal, and cultures as different as Zambia and Thailand, could understand the principles upon which the United States courts make decisions. Hence, their decisions are more than likely to be out of tune with the United States Constitution, legal precedents and informal institutions. The end result would be an increase in the transaction costs of accepting and enforcing ICJ rulings. Next, the administration of criminal justice in the United States is primarily in the hands of the states. This means that 50 state legislatures would have to accept the ICJ. Some might, but most would not. Finally, judges in the United States are either elected (in about half of the states) or appointed by elected representatives. ICJ judges would have no link to the American voter.

John Yoo and Eric Posner (2004) summarized the problem of accepting IJC as a super supreme court as follows: 'As satisfying as it must be to order the world's most powerful nation to violate its constitutional tradition in order to bring its behavior into compliance with a minor international treaty, the ICJ should recognize that it has merely allowed itself to become a forum for attacking the US.'

REFERENCES

Brubaker, E. (1998), 'The common law and the environment: the Canadian Experience', in P. Hill and R. Meiners (eds), *Who Owns the Environment*, New York: Lanham: Rowman & Littlefield.

Greif, A. (1994), 'Cultural beliefs and the organization of society: a historical and theoretical reflection on collectivist and individualist societies', *Journal of Political Economy*, **102**(5), October, 912–57.

Index of Economic Freedom (annual publication), Washington D.C.: Heritage Foundation and *Wall Street Journal*.

Meese, E., M. Spalding and D. Forte (2005), *The Heritage Guide to the Constitution*, Washington, D.C.: Regnery Publishing.

Moser, P. (1994), 'Constitutional protection of economic rights: the Swiss and US experience in comparison', *Constitutional Political Economy*, **5**(1), 61–79.

Pipes, R. (1999), *Property and Freedom*, New York: Alfred Knopf.

Posner, R. (2003), *Economic Analysis of Law*, New York: Aspen Publishers.

Yoo, J. and E. Posner (2004), 'International court of hubris,' *Wall Street Journal*, 7 April.

6. The economic functions of the constitution

In the *Federalist Papers*, no. 51, James Madison, a founding father of the US Constitution, argued that constitutional protection of the rights of individuals must precede the development of all other institutions, including a majority rule. Two centuries later, James Buchanan (1993, p. 59), a Nobel laureate, concurred with Madison, saying that, if individual liberty is to be protected, 'constitutional limits must be in place prior to and separately from any exercise of democratic governance ... "constitutional" must be placed in front of the word "democracy" if the political equality of individuals is to be translated with any meaningful measure of freedom and autonomy' (Buchanan, 1993, p. 59).

Fareed Zakaria, an American political commentator, went one step further. Having noted that many scholars and politicians do applaud the spread of democracies (118 out of 193 countries by the end of the twentieth century), he raised the crucial question: what happens in those countries after elections? One can surely adopt democratic procedures to select the rulers. However, this choice does not necessarily guarantee that, once in power, rulers are committed to the protection of liberty (e.g., Iran and Venezuela in the early 2000s) or that minorities are protected (pick any new country in the Balkans in the late 1990s). Zakaria observed that, in a majority of allegedly democratic countries, citizens may have political rights – that is, the right to select the ruling parties or coalitions – but they have few civic and economic freedoms. Zakaria (1997, pp. 42–3) defined such institutional contexts as illiberal democracies. Like Buchanan, Zakaria argued that democracy without constitutional liberalism leads to the erosion of individual liberty.

Writing about institutional changes in Central and Eastern Europe, Cass Sunstein argued that the term 'constitution' must come before the term 'democracy' in that region. He said (1993, p. 918): 'For Eastern Europe in general the drafting of a constitution [begins] the process of creating a legal culture with firm judicial protection of individual rights ... prominent among them property ownership and freedom of contract.' Some years later, Robert Barro (2000, p. 47) criticized Madeleine Albright for saying that democracy was a prerequisite for economic growth. Barro argued that the rule of law is a major stimulus for economic development.

THE CONSTITUTION IN A RULE OF LAW COUNTRY

In a rule of law country the constitution serves three major objectives, all of them having specific and predictable economic consequences. The constitution has to be the benchmark for all formal laws and regulations; that is, ordinary laws and other rules must be in tune with the basic constitutional principles. The constitution has to protect the rights of individuals from a majority rule. Finally, the constitution has to eliminate or at least substantially contain the discretionary use of power by legislators, bureaucrats and all other public decision makers. To accomplish these objectives, the constitution has to be both credible and stable.

While the concept of the rule of law is rather firmly embedded in the history of Western civilization, different legal systems as well as cultural differences among Western countries have produced different constitutions. And different constitutions have created different behavioral incentives, different transaction costs, and hence the varying attainments of three major objectives. Ed Meese (2005, pp. 2–3), former United States attorney general, explained a major dissimilarity between Anglo-American and Continental legal traditions as follows: 'The consent of the governed stands in contrast to the will of the majority, a view more current in European democracies. The consent of the governed describes a situation where the people are self-governing in their communities, religions, and social institutions, and into which the government may intrude only with the people's consent ... Thus, the limited government is the essential bedrock of the American polity.'

This chapter discusses the United States Constitution of 1787 and the Italian Constitution of 1947/8.[1] The former represents the English liberal tradition, while the latter is an example of the Continental tradition. The chapter incorporates a few references to the Swiss Constitution. The purpose of the discussion is to ascertain the extent to which those constitutions are in tune with the major objectives they are supposed to attain.

THE UNITED STATES CONSTITUTION AND THE DECLARATION OF INDEPENDENCE

The Declaration of Independence and the United States Constitution, the longest surviving written constitution in the world, are the founding documents of the United States of America. The Declaration of Independence defined the philosophical and moral foundations of the United States, while the United States Constitution gave it the structure and the rules for operation. What we know about the founders of the Constitution comes mostly from writing after the fact by friends and foes and should be taken cautiously. The process of ratification of the Constitution was, however, quite interesting and uncertain until the very end.[2]

The following three quotations from the Declaration of Independence define the vision of the Founding Fathers upon which the United States Constitution rests: *We hold these truths to be self-evident* tell us that the Founding Fathers adhered to the tradition of natural law. *The consent of the governed* means that the Founding Fathers wanted the Constitution to be like a contract, rather than like a law. This distinction is important because it affects the costs of changing the document. A contract can be changed only with the consent of all parties to that contract, while a majority (simple or qualified) suffices to change a law. Finally, *all men are created equal*, emphasizes the Founding Fathers' acceptance of the doctrine of natural law, which holds that all men are created equal by nature and independent of governments and prior formal laws.

The United States Constitution sidestepped an important principle spelled out in the Declaration of Independence. The principle of equality was tampered with, for slavery did exist in the United States at the time of the Declaration and at the time of the Constitution. True enough, if the Declaration of Independence had insisted on the abolition of slavery, the Constitution would not have been ratified. The Founding Fathers had to compromise, and only by compromising were they able to create the United States as we know it. Harry Jaffa (2005, pp. 14–15) explained this compromise as follows: 'According to Lincoln, the original Constitution recognized slavery only as a matter of necessity, but not of right ... What was wonderful – nay miraculous – was that a nation of slave holders, on becoming independent, declared that all men are created equal, and thereby made it a moral and political necessity that slavery be abolished.'

Let us now turn to analysis of how and why the United States Constitution serves three major objectives of the rule of law.

The United States Constitution as the Benchmark for Ordinary Laws

In the United States, two key mechanisms for keeping ordinary laws and regulations in tune with the Constitution are the president's power to veto legislative acts of the United States Congress and the process of judicial review discussed in Chapter 5. In addition to those two mechanisms, the executive branches of government, the United States Congress and the states have several legal remedies against rulings by federal judges. They can take a lower court decision to the Supreme Court, they can propose an amendment to the Constitution and the United States Congress and/or the states can enact laws that modify, redefine or slightly change the law deemed unconstitutional by a federal court. The following are a few examples of those remedies.

During the Great Depression in the United States, the US Congress enacted a number of laws. Many of those laws were in direct conflict with both the US

Constitution and prevailing informal rules. Initially, the Supreme Court struck down a number of those laws. In 1935, the Supreme Court invalidated the Railroad Retirement Act, which established a compulsory retirement plan for railroad workers. In the same year, the Supreme Court threw out a law that regulated the wages and hours of slaughterhouse workers in New York. In 1936, it ruled that Congress did not have the power to regulate the relationship between employer and employee. However, under a direct threat from Roosevelt to 'pack' the Court with his lieutenants, the Supreme Court eventually surrendered, and many unconstitutional laws were not challenged (Levin, 2005, pp. 133–5). It was only in the 1980s that the Court began to reverse this trend of going along with the other two branches of government.[3]

Affirmative action programs are governed by a number of federal laws. Their objective is to reduce the effects of racial discrimination. With respect to higher education, the purpose of affirmative action is to encourage universities to increase the enrollment of minorities (primarily African-Americans). In *Hopwood* v *Texas*, four qualified white students were denied admission to the University of Texas School of Law. They sued the university for discrimination in reverse. The argument was that they were rejected in favor of much less qualified students just because those students were blacks. The court agreed. The ruling said that the University of Texas School of Law may not use race as a factor in deciding who is to be admitted (78 F .3d 932, 5th Cir. 1996). Notwithstanding the rules and regulations on this subject by the other two branches of government, the *Hopwood* decision became the law of the land in Louisiana, Mississippi and Texas – the Fifth US Circuit Court of Appeals jurisdiction. Seven years later the Supreme Court partially reversed the Hopwood decision when it ruled that race could be used as a criterion in school admissions. However, the Court said that using any mechanical system, such as quotas, to diversify the student body is unconstitutional (*Gratz* v *Bollinger*, 2003 No 02-516). The ruling was conformed in 2006 (*Parents Involved in Community Schools* v *Seattler School District*, No 05-908)

It is also possible for the states to react to the Supreme Court decisions affecting them. In *Kelo* v *City of New London (2005)* a divided Supreme Court (5–4) ruled that the government can take possession of private property against the owner's will and transfer it to private developers when the result will promote economic development. In writing the majority opinion, Justice John Paul Stevens said: 'Promoting economic development is a traditional and long accepted function of government.' In this case, the Supreme Court said that taking possession of private property to promote economic development is not unconstitutional. But the Supreme Court also left it to the states to determine the method of taking property. Within a few months after the *Kelo* v *City of New London* ruling, more than 30 states have either enacted statutes allowing eminent domain only for traditional purposes (e.g., roads, railroads) or proposed constitutional amendments along the same lines, while most others are in the process of preparing such legislation. Why?

The Supreme Court decision has created uproar in the United States. And it has done so for a very legitimate reason. The United States Constitution does not say that economic development is a function of federal government. The basic premise of the common law is the protection of private property rights. Respect for private property rights is *a given* in the American tradition and customs, and the compensation for taking property, which is based on the current market prices for similar properties in the same area, has nothing in common with the value of property, which depends on the subjective preferences of owners. Moreover, the involuntary transfer of private property to private developers destroys the credibility of private property rights. In this case, the rights of the states vis-à-vis federal government have given the American culture of capitalism a chance to prevail over federal judiciary decisions like *Kelo*.

There is no reason to assume that federal courts will avoid making decisions inconsistent with the Constitution, as the Supreme Court showed in *Kelo v City of New London*. The Public Choice School explains (and human nature underscores) that some court decisions may well be out of tune with the Constitution. The Constitution is valuable not because it is untouchable, which it has not been. It is valuable for a much more important reason. Regardless of how much the Constitution has been eroded, it is the best benchmark against which new formal rules can be evaluated.

The issue for analysis is not whether the US Constitution has been compromised; all constitutions have been compromised at one time or another. The real issue is whether on balance the Constitution has been the benchmark for evaluating laws and regulations. Research and evidence suggest that the US Constitution has performed reasonably well as the benchmark for laws and regulations over a long period of time. In a roundabout way, the *Kelo v City of New London* ruling supports this conclusion.

The United States Constitution as the Guardian of the Rights of Individuals against the Will of the Majority

A change in the United States Constitution has to be approved by two-thirds of both Houses of Congress and ratified by three-fourths of the states. This means that the 13 smallest states, which account for about 6 percent of total population in the United States, can effectively freeze the Constitution. As mentioned, the Founding Fathers made the Constitution 'like a contract' document, in which all parties must agree to changes. In economic jargon, the Founding Fathers raised the transaction costs of changing the Constitution. Indeed, the Constitution has changed only 27 times since 1787.

A major economic consequence of the high costs of changing the United States Constitution is that it softens a prejudice against entrepreneurial decisions that imply long-run commitments and consequences. The weakening of that bias creates incentives for individuals to seek the most beneficial exchange opportunities regardless of their time horizons and, as discussed in Chapter 13, develop the efficiency-friendly institutions. And those incentives reduce the transaction costs of creating new opportunities for exchange and of pursuing existing ones. While not preventing the growth of government, something that no social system has ever done, the contract-like constitution in the United States has done better than those in other Western countries in keeping the private sector of the economy strong and innovative. Phenomena like Bill Gates and John Dell are not happening in the overregulated European Union.

In the United States, the independent judiciary plays an important role in protecting the rights of individuals against the will of the majority. That is why the process of appointment of judges is made at the highest levels of government. All federal judges are nominated by the president and approved by a simple majority of senators. Their appointments are for life. That is, once on the bench, federal judges are independent from other branches of government.[4]

The rules on appointing federal judges, ratifying foreign treaties and electing the president of the United States demonstrate the constitutional protection of smaller states.[5] Regardless of its size, each state has two senators. This means that, in the process of choosing federal judges, California and Wyoming, with populations of about 30 million and 400 000 respectively, have the same number of votes. To put it differently, 400 000 people in Wyoming have the same influence in choosing federal judges as 30 million people in California. The same applies to the ratification of foreign treaties, which have to be ratified by a majority vote in the Senate. And those treaties, including the amount as well as the distribution of foreign aid, have long-run political and economic consequences for the country.[6]

The method of electing the president of the United States is also a good example of the Founding Fathers' respect for state rights. The president is elected by the Electoral College. A party that wins presidential elections in any state (even with a slim majority, as in Florida in 2000) controls the entire delegation of electors from that state. The number of electors from a state is equal to the number of its elected members of the House of Representatives plus its two senators. This means that two states with populations of 400 000 each will participate with six votes in the process of electing the president of the United States (one representative and two senators from each state). At the same time, another state with a population of 800 000 has a total of four electors (two representatives and two senators). Two smaller states with the same population as that of a bigger state thus have two more votes on the board of electors. To change the system of electing the president would require an amendment to the

United States Constitution. Since the probability that the 13 smallest states with about 6 percent of the total population would ratify such an amendment is close to zero, it is quite likely that the constitutional protection that people in small states have against majority rule in the process of electing the United States president will continue well into the future.

The Constitution clearly meant to make the United States not a democracy but a union of sovereign states. Are they as sovereign today as the Founders wanted them to be? They are not. However, the appointment of judges, the selection of presidents and the ratification of treaties are a few examples demonstrating that the Founding Fathers' preference for states' rights vis-à-vis the federal government and for the protection of small states from big ones is still alive in the United States. Moreover, laws governing business firms, education, crimes and family matters are still the province of the states. That is, their laws and regulations have not been 'harmonized' by federal government.[7] The states have their own tax systems. The state of Texas does not have state income tax, while New York has it. In all, 27 states elect state judges, but in other states the judges are nominated by governors and approved by state senators.

Constitutional Protection from the Discretionary Use of Power

To constrain the discretionary use of power by the federal government, the Founding Fathers relied on (1) the dispersion of power between the three branches of the federal government: executive, legislative and judicial; the principle of enumerated powers for federal government; and (2) the separation of powers between federal government and the states.

James Madison was well aware of the importance of the dispersion of powers among the three branches of government. He wrote (*Federalist Papers*, no. 47). 'The preservation of liberty requires that the three great departments of power should be separate and distinct [because] the accumulation of all powers, legislative, executive, and judiciary, in the same hand, whether of one, a few, or many, and whether hereditary, self-appointed or elective, may justly be pronounced the very definition of tyranny.'

The principle of enumerated powers means that executive and federal branches of federal government can pursue only those activities that are specifically enumerated in the Constitution: according to the tenth amendment, all activities not explicitly given to federal government belong to the states and/or individual citizens. And James Madison wrote in *The Federalist Papers*, no.45, 'The powers delegated by the Constitution to the Federal government are few and defined [while] those which are to remain in the States are numerous and indefinite.'

The tenth amendment has been abused more often than any other article of the United States Constitution. The Security and Exchange Commission, the

Department of Education and the Department of Human Resources are only a few among many examples of federal government assuming powers not delegated to it by the Constitution. The word 'abortion' does not even appear in the Constitution, which means that the Supreme Court should have left the issue of abortion to be decided by the states. The Constitution does not contain any reference to social justice; it is all about state rights, individual liberty and private property. Yet we have many senators and representatives defending their subjective perceptions of social justice by reference to the Constitution.

While the balance of power has been shifting away from the states and in favor of the federal government since the Great Depression in the 1930s, Supreme Court decisions began to change the trend, however slightly, in the late 1970s and early 1980s. The Reagan Administration relaxed antitrust rulings. The Supreme Court began to pay attention to the effects of legal rulings on the economy, which translates into a greater protection of the states and property rights. It even cited the Chicago School in making a decision (Kovacic and Shapiro, 2000). Early indications are that the Roberts Court might stop or at least slow down the transfer of power from the states to the federal government. For example, the Supreme Court sided with home builders over environmentalists, agreeing that the state of Arizona could take over clean-water enforcement without first being reviewed by the federal Fish and Wildlife Service (no. 06-340, July 27, 2007). This decision does not mean that the Justices are not concerned with environmental issues. It means, however, that the Justices think that some issues are better decided on a state-by-state basis.

An important fact is that the Supreme Court can change the balance of power in favor of the states at a lower cost than can the other two branches of federal government. It is less costly (in terms of time, resources and prestige) for the justices of the Supreme Court to increase state rights by the strict application of the tenth amendment than to make rulings that increase the power of the federal government. That is so because rulings in support of the latter require a 'convincing interpretation' of the constitutionality of those rulings. And, as in the *Kelo* case, a substantial loss of prestige for the Court is the real cost to be borne by the justices themselves. In short, incentives and transaction costs of federal judges favor 'going along' with the Constitution.

Social Forces Supportive of the United States Constitution

Why have several generations of Americans accepted a constitution that binds the present to the past? A plausible explanation lies in the fact that, before reaching North America, most Western European settlers were at the margin of the hierarchic structures prevailing in their own regions, both in the Church and in the secular domain. It was therefore apparent to most pioneers that on the new continent there was little room for class privileges, blind loyalty to traditions, or fear of new ideas. For the first time in human history, hundreds of thousands of people had an opportunity to pursue their individual preferences, take responsibility for their own actions and, in the process, create a new way of life. The American tradition is then the tradition of individualism. The very constraints the Founding Fathers chose to write into the Constitution reflected their commitment to classical liberalism and methodological individualism.

In that sense, the United States Constitution differs from many European constitutions. It emphasizes the process of voluntary exchange, open markets and limited government, while European constitutions tend to be outcome-oriented and thus more amenable to *dirigisme*. Leading American legal scholar Richard Epstein (2004, p. 31) said the following about the proposed EU constitution shortly before its fiasco in 2005:

> [The proposed EU] Constitution allows for such dominance at the center that it will take a political miracle for that competition to play a powerful role in the affairs of the EU. By giving rights with one hand and taking them away with the other, this proposed EU Constitution lacks any clear definition and structure ... But when the dust settles, there will be more government and less freedom for all ... My recommendation is therefore this: opt for the economic free trade zone and consign the EU Constitution to the dust heap.

His remarks could have been directed at most living constitutions in Western Europe in the early twenty-first century.

HISTORY AND DEVELOPMENT OF THE ITALIAN CONSTITUTION[8]

As discussed in the previous sections, the American Constitution was conceived in a society where individual freedom was held in the utmost esteem. Its purpose was to maintain the colonies united enough to fight a war and open enough to allow free trade. All other aims, such as pursuing national or federal interests, were ruled out. More precisely, the Constitution was designed to guarantee freedom from interference. Had it been about policies, it would have been contrary to the culture of the time and would have stood no chance of being accepted, let alone enforced.

The 1848 Statuto

Continental Europe went through different experiences, so that different rules of the game came to the surface. The Italian 1947/48[9] Constitution provides a good example in this regard, with substantial economic implications. Until 1947, the Italian Basic Law was the Statuto, which had been conceded in 1848 by Charles Albert, King of Sardinia.[10] In theory, the Statuto was aimed at transferring legislative power from the monarch to Parliament (and safeguarding the interests of the bourgeoisie). To compensate for the drive to curb royal discretionary rule making, it was acknowledged that the throne would encompass the executive and judicial powers, and act as the guarantor of both law-and-order and individual freedoms. That explains why the Statuto was indeed conceived as a Constitution, in that it defined the rules of the game and shied away from prescribing policy purposes. As regards flexibility, at the very beginning some political actors (including Count Cavour) stuck to the fact that it was a royal law rather than a parliamentary law. Therefore, they were persuaded that it had some sort of a super-status and that it could be modified by the king only.

In fact, the rules it established could be elaborated upon with relative ease, and thus provided enough flexibility to accommodate both the intense struggles that characterized Italian political life from the mid-nineteenth century and the expansion of the state.[11] Accountability to the people was not part of the game. Similarly, the Statuto did not aim at uniting the country but rather at shaping a new role for the monarchy, and providing an attractive institutional framework to lure the elites of the new regions that the Sardinian King was eager to annex (unification under a constitutional monarch had a better sound than conquest by an absolute sovereign).

As we know, in the end things did not evolve as some of the main actors had predicted. The King gradually lost ground, for the Italian Parliament was quick to extend its legitimacy to legislate on statutory matters as well, and to claim that it was 'always constituent, and constituted'. From the 1850s, Parliament took advantage of the fact that the King was relatively weak and his key charismatic supporter – Cavour – no longer at his side. It did not take long for law making to degenerate into widespread rent seeking fueled by powerful, organized interest groups, which the classical–liberal elements contained in the Statuto hardly stopped.[12] In the end, as the various groups tried to get the upper hand by relying to an increasing extent on popular sentiments, they de facto paved the way for the twentieth-century demagogic dynamics, and oligarchic rule soon gave in to populism. Not surprisingly, when the first World War finally added its nationalistic coat, and in 1922 Mussolini made his amateurish (but successful) attempt to grab power, the King failed or refused to perceive the implications, did not enforce the Statuto, and gave in.

The Republican Constitution

Having arrested Mussolini in July 1943, the King pretended that he was restoring the legal framework consistent with the letter of the Statuto. But, of course, in 1943, things were not the same as in 1922. The King had lost credibility and his conduct during 1943–45 further diminished his chances of steering transition from a dictatorship to a multi-party democratic system.

The Statuto had acquired negative symbolic connotations. It had provided the context within which the monarchy had given in to Fascism and – more generally – it was identified with a past that everybody agreed to pretend belonged to somebody else.[13] As early as October 1943, the leaders of most anti-fascist parties formally declared the need for a new constitution.[14] The content of a new constitutional moment went beyond symbols, though. It was to be made clear that the new constitutional rules were coming from 'below'. In fact, the Republican Constitution was conceived as an instrument through which a partially new ruling elite could obtain, hold and share power. The race began soon after the downfall of Fascism in 1943, when different political formations had tried to legitimize their ambitions through the so-called Resistenza (partisan guerilla against the German occupants and Mussolini's puppet state in northern Italy). Despite acute tensions among the various factions, the elites of those political parties – including the communists – agreed to remove the King and to share power more or less following democratic rules.[15] This was already manifest in June 1944, when the government resigned and the parties took over without consulting the King, in patent violation of the Statuto, which was of course still in force at that moment. Churchill was well aware of what this meant, but he finally decided to turn a blind eye and recognize the new government as legitimate. By doing so he effectively let the King down and sided with the reformers of the coalesced parties (Novacco, 2000, pp. 29–30).

True enough, these new rules were not going to be submitted to the people for approval, perhaps to save 'the Assembly from the possible embarrassment of having the voters reject the Constitution it had approved, as had occurred in France shortly before' (Adams and Barile, 1953, p. 63). Still, leaders across the political spectrum went a long way to persuade the population that such rules were 'just and anti-fascist' and therefore to be shared with no need for further debates or consultation.

Perhaps more important, people had to be convinced that, by means of a suitably conceived party system, power could be attained by everybody. Close association with the traditional elites, such as the monarchy or the very top brass of the fascist party, was no longer a prerequisite. This clarifies why the Republican Constitution repeatedly paid lip service to populist slogans dear to the Left. For instance, article 1 suggests that only the labour class (workers) enjoys constitutional rights; article 46 prescribes the Illyrian model (joint management by workers and shareholders) as the ideal entrepreneurial format.[16] And it also explains why this Constitution devoted little attention to the protection of the individual against abuse by politicians and bureaucrats, but made a deliberate effort to fragment power across different layers and jurisdictions, so as to enhance more rent-seeking opportunities for the party members and disperse individual responsibilities.

As mentioned earlier, and contrary to what happened in other countries, in Italy it was soon agreed that the center of political life was to be the party system. The real leaders were and would be the secretaries of the parties – not the prime minister or the president of the republic. Thus, new rules of the game had to be created to that effect.[17] As a result, the primary aim of the Italian Constituent Fathers was not to identify the fundamental principles that would limit abuse by the state, but rather to discover ways to prevent some political parties from oppressing other political parties and to encourage coalition governments, rather than effective authority (Novacco, 2000). Put differently, the social criteria mentioned in the Republican Constitution involve the balance of power among political parties. Each alleged 'principle' prescribed by that Basic Law should therefore be read as a limit to the actions of the governing coalitions, or at least as an instrument to prevent hegemonic rule. The individual who is the pillar of the classical–liberal rule-of-law system remains out of the picture.

This explains why, from a classical–liberal standpoint, the Republican Constitution was a partial success as regards the packaging, but a failure in terms of substance. It was a success since it turned out to be a fairly stable super-law, even if its rigidity made sure that the features of the particular historical moment that generated the Constitution were never really overcome in later years. In addition, its rather complex system of checks and balances made sure that nobody could concentrate much power. On the other hand, success was partial, for it offered only weak protection to individual liberty (freedom from coercion and encroachment by the state). And the price to be paid in order to build up a party-ruled regime (compromise[18] and consensus building at the expense of personal freedom and consistency) continued to be paid even when breaking away from Fascism ceased to be an issue.

To conclude, the first Italian Constitution (the Statuto) was an attempt to regulate the assignment of power between a relatively weak monarchy and an increasingly strong liberal elite. Instead, the Italian Republican Constitution represented an example of vicious path dependence induced by a shock – the downfall of fascist nationalism – to which a cooperative rent-seeking solution was offered. The constitutional rules of 1947–48 were effective in that they changed the structure of power, avoided potential armed confrontation and provided an arena where personal ambitions could be developed (but also neutralized). Still, to an extent, they confirmed and legitimized the experience of the 1920s and 1930s, when individual rights were violated and outcome-oriented law making in the collective interest was common.[19]

THE HISTORY AND DEVELOPMENT OF THE SWISS CONSTITUTION

The birth of the Swiss Confederation is usually identified with the 1291 pact signed by three communities/cantons (the *Waldstätten*), which agreed to establish a military alliance against the Hapsburg feudal lords and claimed independence or direct submission to the emperor. It turned out to be a success story. As early as 1318, the *Waldstätten* were already treated as equals by their neighbors: although those three cantons did not consider themselves parts of a state, they were definitely regarded as a military power to be reckoned with and a worthy counterpart in international matters.

This military alliance gradually widened: it accepted new cantons, forced new communities to join as equals, and also increased its boundaries by annexing new territories, where the populations were treated as subjects. Of course, at that time freedom and democracy were not part of the agenda. It was a question of survival from a military and an economic standpoint.

These were the founding features of the confederation. They remained roughly constant for over 500 years, during which each canton carried on its own policies. Conflicts among cantons were frequent, sometimes even at the risk of breaking apart the confederation. Some attempts were made to stop inter-canton aggression, such as through the Covenants of Sempach (1393), but turmoil and disintegration were looming. In a word, the Swiss were facing two 'constitutional' problems: they had to find out how to deal with secession and with internicine wars. It turned out that, in both cases, the solution was military confrontation, followed by compromise. Nobody ever mentioned natural laws, individual rights or other philosophical matters.

The first serious secession crisis came in the 1440s, when the Confederates denied Zürich the right to leave the alliance, fought against the 'rebel' city, and won. Another episode of civil war took place in the late 1470s, when the peasant communities feared expansion by the urbanized cantons. The result was the compromise of Stans (1481), a treaty that bound its signatories to behave according to agreed rules of conduct under more or less well-defined circumstances. But the typical canton continued to remain similar to a sovereign state ruled by local oligarchies. This principle was affirmed once again with particular vigor in the seventeenth century, especially by the Catholic communities, which feared for their autonomy if federal principles were to be introduced and applied.[20] There was no moral principle with which to comply, no common will to pursue, other than joining forces for defensive and offensive purposes.

Contrary to the American and the Italian situations, the first Swiss constitutional project was not the result of external aggression, domestic power struggle among elites, or national catastrophes. Instead, it was the consequence of an attempt to leave the alliance, an effort to deny the right to secede (this time to the Catholic cantons, the *Sonderbund*) and a civil war (1847). After defeat, in 1848, the *Sonderbund* cantons were required to fall into line and accept the status quo ante, pay a fine (later partially written off), contribute to the allied army and abstain from blockading rival cantons. In addition, the winners imposed a federal constitution, so as to eliminate secession at its roots.[21]

In accordance with Swiss tradition and spirit, although the 1848 Constitution proclaimed the Confederation as a national state, it did not destroy the independence of the cantons. Rather it was introduced as little more than an agreement to regulate matters of common interest, to promote free trade within the Confederation and to protect the traditional rules of the game, including the cantonal constitutions. Oligarchic traditions were manifest in the seven-member Federal Council (the government), while popular sovereignty was confirmed through mechanisms of direct democracy (referenda). But the crucial political tools to enhance the role of the state were also put in place: the legislative powers were entrusted to one chamber (the National Council) elected by the people, and one chamber (the State Council) with two representatives for each canton – comparable to the American system.

Not surprisingly, once the confederated state was formally recognized and its institutions started to function, centralization became a matter of time.[22] Today the cantons are regions that have indeed preserved their own taxing power as well as autonomy in various domains, such as education and police.[23] But harmonization is pervasive: federal taxation currently accounts for some 45 percent of total fiscal revenues, while the cantons take 32 percent and the Municipalities 23 percent.[24] More generally, economic policy became recognized as an area of federal relevance by the late 1940s, when the federal welfare state was created. These phenomena intensified further in the second part of the twentieth century, as a consequence of path dependence and public-choice mechanisms; and also as a result of increased mobility, which considerably weakened the sentiment of cantonal loyalty.[25]

But the initial purpose (a peace treaty enforcing a military alliance) has remained in place. To be sure, today the Constitution itself does not seem to play a great role in the political heart of the Swiss people: having been revised some 140 times since 1848 – thereby effectively transforming Switzerland from a confederation into what some have been calling a 'Cooperative Federation' (Béguin, 1980, p. 361)[26] – the 'new' Constitution was approved in April 1999 by only 21 percent of the Swiss. And rightly so, perhaps, for in the Swiss case the bulwarks of the rule of law are cantonal independence and direct democracy, to which the Constitution is subject (rather than the other way around).

CONCLUSION

This chapter has defined the constitution and identified its major objectives. It then proceeded to establish the extent to which constitutions in a common law country such as the United States and civil code countries such as Italy and Switzerland serve those general constitutional objectives and ultimately contribute to defining the position of those countries vis-à-vis the concept of the rule of law.

The findings for the United States Constitution were (a) the high costs of changing the Constitution explain its stability over a period of more than two hundred years; (b) the Constitution has been the benchmark for laws and regulations. This is not to say that the Constitution has not been tampered with; however, it has provided a useful and effective yardstick for the questioning of proposed laws and regulations; (c) competition between the three branches of federal government, competition between the states, and competition between the states and the federal government, with some predictable ups and downs, has protected individuals against majority rule.

The Swiss Constitution has been drafted along similar lines. Although the emphasis on individual liberties is less pronounced, its history has made sure that sovereignty remained deeply rooted with the people and with the cantons, each of which has its own constitution. That provided an effective shield against arbitrary policy making, which can be kept in check by the cantons. However, emphasis on referenda rather than judicial review of new formal rules makes the protection of minorities inadequate. The lack of an opting-out prospect has allowed the federal politicians to extend their powers. Still, the speed of this process has been considerably slowed by their being accountable to the people (direct democracy) rather than to themselves (parliamentary democracy).

This contrasts sharply with the Italian experiences. First, the 1848 Statuto was conceived as the instrument whereby the king planned to buy off interest groups, not to guarantee the rule of law.[27] The soft underbelly in the Statuto was the idea of concentrating powers in the hands of a king who turned out to be unwilling to use them, possibly weakened by his own lack of legitimacy or by his refusal to rely on popular support to fight the rising elites. The 1947/48 Republican Constitution was also indifferent to individual freedom and local autonomy, for these items were not on the agenda when the fascist regime collapsed and new political elites claimed power. In the end, the alleged shortcomings of the Statuto were answered by creating a host of new competing beneficiaries, rather than by conceiving a new vision.[28]

As time went by it became clear that the Italian Constitution had not been conceived to protect individual rights, since it dealt with the common good, to be defined by ordinary policy making. In fact, although it is commonly perceived as a super-law, the Republican Constitution has now turned out to be rather flexible outside the procedural domain, and, when asked to interpret its 'true' spirit, the Constitutional Court has tended to adopt or extend the notions of collective interest and social justice, following shared perceptions and the (somewhat wavering) common will, rather than following well-defined principles derived from informal rules (tradition, customs, religion, etc.).

NOTES

1. The Italian Constitution was voted by Parliament in December 1947 and went into effect in January 1948.
2. The Declaration of Independence was enacted on 4 July 1776 in Philadelphia. The Constitutional Convention met from May to September 1787 in Philadelphia. In September, the Constitution was sent to the original 13 states for ratification. The first state to ratify the Constitution was Delaware (7 December 1787) and Rhode Island was the last (29 May 1790). But the outcome was up in the air until the very end.
3. See E. Kovacic and C. Shapiro (2000), 'Antitrust policy: a century of economic and legal thinking', *Journal of Economic Perspectives*, **14**, 43–60.
4. Indeed, many judges who were considered conservative at the time of their appointment eventually turned out to be quite liberal (left of center in American political jargon), and vice versa.
5. The US Congress has two houses, the House of Representatives and the Senate. Each state has two senators regardless of the size of its population. The number of representatives the states send to Washington depends on the size of their respective population. One representative is elected for every 400 000 people or fraction thereof. A major function of the House is to capture changes in preferences of the median voter. A major function of the Senate is to protect the tradition upon which the US Constitution rests.
6. The House of Representatives, which is based on one man one vote, has no voice in either the approval of judges or the ratification of foreign treaties.
7. This is not to say that federal government has given up on harmonizing laws and regulations. The Sarbanes–Oxley Act represents one such attempt to violate the tenth amendment by using the bankruptcy of Enron as an excuse.
8. Enrico Colombatto, professor of economics at the University of Turin and director of the Center for International Economic Research wrote the sections on Italian and Swiss constitutions.
9. The Italian Constitution was drafted by an ad hoc Constitutional Assembly. It was approved by Parliament in December 1947 and entered into effect on 1 January 1948. It is still in force today, with minor changes with respect to its original formulation.
10. Until 1859, the Kingdom of Sardinia also included Piedmont, Genoa, Nice and Savoy. The capital was Turin. It became the Kingdom of Italy in 1861.
11. Although the Statuto provided little opposition to modification of the rules, the law maker was still obliged to operate on new versions of the existing rules: 'the Italian Constitution which was enacted at its origin has become cumulative in its development' (Arangio Ruiz, 1895, p. 227).
12. Article 25 prescribed the 'flat tax', article 26 individual freedom, article 29 claimed that 'no form of property can be infringed upon', article 30 that 'all forms of taxation must be allowed by Parliament and approved by the King'.
13. In June 1946, the Christian Democrats and the Communists agreed on condoning all crimes committed by fascists as well as by partisans over the previous years. Following Novacco (2000, p. 91), this explains why the (fascist) bureaucracy remained loyal to the Christian Democrats during the post-Second World War era, while the Socialists lost ground, never to recover (the socialist leader Pietro Nenni had opposed all kinds of pardon).
14. Opposition came from the monarchists, who rightly feared that a constitutional break would

also imply a shift towards a republican regime (the King was voted out in June 1946) and from conservative quarters, who feared a leap into the unknown, which could possibly have strong communist traits.

15. Not surprisingly, the monarchic partisans were not part of the republican piece of the deal.

16. Nevertheless, the Constitutional Assembly succeeded in weakening the Marxist thrust that had characterized the first months following the end of the war. As shown by Einaudi (1948, pp. 662–63), the communist features typical of the preliminary drafts were quietly put aside as the preparatory work went along. Part of the 'success' was also due to the way the Constituent Assembly decided to proceed. It included 556 members. Some of them did almost nothing. Others were assigned by the parties to various sub-committees, each of them in charge of elaborating sections of the Constitution, to be submitted for approval to the general assembly. As reported by Adams and Barile (1953, p. 62), the Christian Democrats took care of the rights and duties of the citizens, the Communists were assigned to the organization of the state, while the Socialists drafted the articles regarding social and economic matters.

17. This agreement held true even when Italy officially became associated with the 'Western bloc' and tension between the Left and the other parties became acute (May 1947). Note that the Constituent Assembly had been elected one year earlier (June 1946) and that the Constitution was still a 'work in progress'.

18. Caianiello (2002) recalls that the Republican Constitution includes parts of the pre-fascist conservative tradition, the contribution of left-wing elitist ideologies, Catholic and Marxist moral principles. Everybody could claim to be the moral winner of the 'Resistenza'. Tellingly enough, there is no reference to the classical–liberal tradition. See also Adams and Barile (1953), who point out some contradictions that were soon exploited by Parliament in ordinary law making.

19. Of course, whereas during Fascism the collective interest meant nationalism and a relatively modest welfare state, the republic proposed a notion of collective interest composed of extensive redistribution and social justice: article 2 of the constitution emphasizes that all citizens are required to comply with the principles of political, economic and social solidarity; article 3 claims that the state must provide the means to develop the personality of each citizen; article 4 argues that all citizens have the duty to contribute to the common good. All notions of freedom are restricted to the realm of politics (Part I), not of economics. This is not an accident, for private initiative and private property are subject to and serve the common good (articles 41 and 42).

20. For centuries, even the well-known Swiss neutrality has been both an imposition of foreign powers (each power would promise not to invade Switzerland as long as the Swiss undertook not to support potential enemies) and the result of the Confederates' unwillingness to decide on a common foreign policy.

21. This was partly due to the fact that the *Sonderbund* war had ended with the total defeat of the 'rebels'. As a result, the vanquished knew well they were at the mercy of the winners. Thus, they perceived the winners' constitutional proposal as a generous deal. It should also be observed that the fight had been short and bloodless, so that bad feelings did not go very deep. The same could not have happened in the USA at the end of the Civil War.

22. Moser (1994) compares the US and the Swiss Constitutions, to conclude that 'both constitutions rely on rather different strategies to protect economic liberties – with limited success in both cases ... the regulation of trade and business by the cantons has expanded considerably ... and, in 1971, it introduced *social policy motivations* as a new reason for permitting intervention in the freedom to trade' (pp. 62, 71).

23. That accounts for the wide difference in maximum tax rates on personal income, which in 2002 ranged from over 45 percent in Geneva and Jura to 25 percent or lower in Schwyz and Zug (Cuomo, 2004). It also explains both the high degree of fiscal decentralization of Switzerland compared to Europe (Curzon Price and Garello, 2003, p. 450) and this country's relatively high degree of economic freedom.

24. In particular, consumption taxes and VAT are exclusive federal responsibility. Similar comments apply to regulation, which the new Constitution assigns to an increasingly large extent to the federal authorities (see, for instance, Viviani and Paola 2005, pp. 112–13).

25. When the Swiss started to move around and settle outside their original cantons, the idea of

competing cantonal welfare states was quickly replaced by the notion of a federal welfare state. The percentage of Swiss citizens living inside their canton of origin fell below 50 percent in the early 1980s.

26. At the moment there exist over 300 Agreements between the cantons and the Confederation.

27. Contrary to the common claim that Italy lacked the traditions to produce popular sovereignty (see, for instance, Arangio Ruiz, 1895, p. 39), it has been here argued that the rules of the game introduced by the Statuto involved a different notion of sovereign popularity and were designed to attain different goals.

28. Indeed, Adams and Barile (1953, p. 64) maintain that the Republican Constitution was not substantially different from the Statuto: 'in spite of the formally effective new Constitution, Italy is actually being governed under much the same laws, and people, as during Fascism' (p. 83).

REFERENCES

Adams, J. and P. Barile (1953), 'The implementation of the Italian Constitution', *American Political Science Review*, **47**(1), March, 61–83.

Arangio, R. (1895), 'The amendments to the Italian Constitution', *Annals of the American Academy of Political and Social Science*, **6**, September, 31–57.

Barro, R. (2000), 'Rule of law, democracy, and economic performance', *2000 Index of Economic Freedom,* Washington: D.C.: Heritage Foundation and *Wall Street Journal.*

Béguin, P (1980), 'L'histoire récente', in William Martin, *Histoire de la Suisse*, Lausanne: Payot, pp. 319–420.

Buchanan, J. (1993), *Property as a Guarantor of Liberty*, Aldershot, UK and Brookfield, US: Edward Elgar.

Caianiello, V. (2002), 'La Costituzione Italiana', interview released in Rome on 30 April, downloaded from http://www.emsf.rai.it/grillo/trasmissioni.asp?d=908.

Cuomo, A. (2004), 'Les grandes lignes du régime fiscal suisse', *IREF*, May.

Curzon, P. and J. Garello (2003), 'Index of fiscal decentralization. Methodology and findings', *Journal des Économistes et des Études Humaines*, **13**(4), Décembre, pp. 441–78.

Einaudi, M (1948), 'The constitution of the Italian Republic', *American Political Science Review*, **42**(4), August, 661–76.

Epstein, R. (2004), 'American lessons for European federalism: doubts about the proposed EU Constitution', lecture presented at the *Cass Business School*, London, 14 October.

Jaffa, H. (2005), 'The false prophets of American conservatism: Rehnquist and Scalia', paper presented at annual meeting of the American Political Science Association, September, the Claremont Institute, Claremont (California).

Kovacic, W. and C. Shapiro (2000), 'Antitrust policy: a century of economic and legal thinking', *Journal of Economic Perspectives*, **14**(1), 43–60.

Levin, Mark (2005), *Men in Black*, Washington, DC: Regnery Publishing.

Meese, E. (2005), 'The meaning of the constitution', in E. Meese, D. Forte and M. Spalding (eds), *The Heritage Guide to the Constitution*, Washington D.C.: Regnery, pp. 1–6.

Moser, P. (1994), 'Constitutional protection of economic rights: the Swiss and US experience in comparison', *Constitutional Political Economy*, **12**, Winter, 61–79

Novacco, D. (2000), *L'Officina della Costituzione Italiana*, Milan: Feltrinelli.

Sunstein, C. (1993), 'On property and constitutionalism', *Cardozo Law Review*, **14**(3), 907–35.

Viviani, S. and M. Paola (2005), 'Federalismo e Regionalismo in Svizzera. Recenti Sviluppi', in Alessandra Lang and Cecilia Sanna (eds), *Federalismo e Regionalismo*, Milan: Giuffré, pp. 107–16.

Zakaria, F. (1997), 'The rise of illiberal democracy', *Foreign Affairs*, November–December, 22–43.

7.   Private property rights

Early in the twentieth century, Irvin Fisher (1916, p. 27) wrote: 'A property right is the liberty or permit to enjoy benefits of wealth ... while assuming the costs which those benefits entail.' The Fisher quotation is quite consistent with the way most cultures, religions, Roman law and common law have thought of property rights. We can say that property rights define *relations among men that arise from the fact of scarcity and pertain to the access to scarce goods*.

From the dawn of human history, individuals have appreciated the importance of property rights for their survival. Primitive men fough each other for the right of access to better caves; tribes claimed property rights in the area where fishing or hunting were good; great religions wrestled with the issue of reconciling the behavioral incentives of property rights with their moral teachings (e.g., usury laws); and a struggle between two different concepts of property rights, as represented by capitalism and socialism, consumed the entire twentieth century.

Social scientists also recognized the importance of property rights. However, it was only in the 1960s that a systematic study of property rights began in the earnest. Armen Alchian, Ronald Coase, Harold Demsetz, Henry Manne, Douglass North and Oliver Williamson, among others, translated the centuries of awareness of the importance of property rights into the economic theory of property rights.

The legal foundation of private property rights had developed in Rome, long before capitalism was born. Roman law specified many types of property rights, including the three types that are still with us. They are private property rights, communal ownership and state (public) ownership. To quote Justinian (Epstein, 1994, p. 24): 'Some things are by natural law common to all, some are public, some belong to a society ... But most things belong to individuals, being acquired by various titles.'

Two examples of the relationship between changes in property rights and economic performance are worth noting because they predate the rise of capitalism. In the early days of the Roman Republic, the prevailing form of ownership in land was the *ager publicus*, whereby land was accessible to all the groups of citizens who wanted to use it.[1] It made economic sense, for cattle-rearing was the main economic activity, while agriculture was developed in very small land parcels (called *heredium*) that were the private property of the citizens.[2] As Rome began to expand in the fifth century BC, and new land was acquired for the *ager publicus*, two new phenomena came to the surface. As better land was conquered, farming became profitable. However, the patrician families contin- ued to be more interested in cattle raising, conducted by their slaves and *clientes*. In short, while the plebeian families perceived the advantages of shifting from cattle raising to farming, which required some forms of long-term investment and thus the privatization of the public land (*agri divisi et adsignati*), the aris- tocrats insisted on having collective ownership of the land, which they had de facto occupied with their herds. The problem was solved to the plebeians' ad- vantage some time in the fifth century BC.[3] They won because they had clearly perceived that the cost of fighting for private ownership was lower than the benefits to be had from intensive farming, while the aristocrats had perceived the possibility of accumulating new wealth through conquest – as long as peace at home was guaranteed, at the cost of giving up archaic privileges.

According to Douglass North (1988) at the beginning of the sixteenth century, institutional arrangements in England and Spain were similar and so were their respective levels of economic development. The wool trade was a major source of royal revenues in both countries. However, the relative security of property rights was not the same, and economic development proceeded along different paths in England and in Spain. In England, prevailing statutes covered only the existing industries, so that new industries were not bound by old rules. More- over, law enforcement in the countryside was in the hands of judges, who were not paid by the crown. Predictably, new industries moved into the countryside where guilds were much weaker, and price and wage controls were not effec- tively enforced. As a consequence, property rights in the countryside were more secure. The result was the spontaneous development of joint-stock companies and growing resentment against crown-sponsored monopolies. Eventually, po- litical power shifted from the crown to Parliament. Toward the end of the seventeenth century, common law replaced old statutes as the law of the land. By helping to replace statutes with common law, competition among various courts with overlapping jurisdiction contributed to more secure property rights and local political controls. All of that helped to enhance economic growth in England (North and Weingast, 1989).

Spain, in contrast, was always characterized by a strong centralized monarchy, which depended on gold and silver shipped from the New World, taxes paid by the sheepherders' guild, and sales taxes. Not surprisingly, property rights were assigned with the purpose of preserving the supremacy of the monarch and of handing out privileges in exchange for loyalty. In return for the right of sheep owners to move their flocks around the country from one area of suitable pasture to another, guilds guaranteed the king a stable flow of income. Consequences of this arrangement were insecure property rights in land and the absence of incentives to prevent soil erosion, both of which arrested economic development (North, 1988).

THE MORALITY OF PRIVATE PROPERTY RIGHTS

As economists we are concerned with the effects of different property rights on economic efficiency and economic development. However, for background purposes, this section touches upon a plausible explanation of the morality of private property rights.

In the Garden of Eden the notion of property was rather simple: everything was owned by the Central Authority, God. He had created the world; thus He owned it, and all creatures were to follow His will. Although one may wonder why God would have wanted to give life to creatures that might not comply with His conception of the world, God had the power to enforce the rules, as Lucifer and his supporters found out.

Such an assignment of property rights was not enough to create economic activities, though, for scarcity was ruled out. Adam and Eve were supposed to be perfectly happy with what God had bestowed upon them at no cost, and they had no incentive to satisfy unmet needs, for there were no unmet needs. As a result, there was neither production nor exchange: everything was available at zero (opportunity) cost.[4]

It is arguable that the original Garden-of-Eden arrangement broke down because God had overlooked the possibility that some inhabitants might choose to acquire new knowledge and might possibly find out about the existence of yet undreamt of needs. Indeed, the never satisfied desire to acquire knowledge is what distinguishes human beings from animals (and from angels).

However, God remained the original owner of everything He had created. Thus, once we became free to choose, the key element that transforms a natural good into a valuable output is the action of mixing man's work with God's endowment. As long as 'man's work' reflects the effort of one individual, that individual alone has honored God. The rights on the output thus obtained are then restricted to the two parties involved – God and the individual. In short, property is private and sacred, and *a fortiori* legitimate (moral). This view is likewise reflected in the classical tradition, where property was also sacred as long as property established the link between God and the individual or the family (Liggio and Chafuen, 2004). This approach also forms the foundation of John Locke's strictest view of property.

Justification for the attenuation of property rights in capitalist countries is usually based on moral grounds or externalities. The former is common in the Continental version of capitalism, where the state is supposed to cooperate with the private sector in promoting economic policies consistent with the public interest and/or the common good as defined by the prevailing ruling group (this definition may change with the outcome of elections). For instance, German law protects property rights only to the extent that they serve 'human dignity' (as if free markets were not doing precisely that) and the welfare state.[5] Property rights in Italy are also attenuated, as the Italian Constitution allows protection of private property insofar as it serves a social function.[6] By failing to protect the subjective preferences of their owners, the incentive effects of property rights in Germany and Italy do not block legislative and regulatory redistributive measures. In short, they offer property owners weaker protection from legislative and regulatory redistributive measures than they might.

The Anglo-American view puts more emphasis on the protection of individual liberty and the enforcement of private property rights. Thus, when the Anglo-American tradition moves away from strict property-right enforcement, it refers to cases when the transaction costs of defining property rights are high relative to potential benefits (Buchanan and Stubblebine, 1962). When benefits change and property rights are defined, externalities disappear. For example, for many decades, most countries claimed only three miles offshore as their territorial waters. The costs of claiming more ocean for themselves were high (e.g., they required more patrol boats) relative to benefits. As the importance of fishing rose and oil discoveries were made offshore, the costs of claiming more ocean fell relative to benefits, and countries changed their boundaries. Territorial seas now reach out 12 miles.

PRIVATE PROPERTY RIGHTS: FROM CUSTOMS TO LAW

Following medieval tradition, the land, gold, silver and other precious resources that European explorers and conquerors encountered and commandeered in South America became the private property of their kings. However, Europeans who went to North America claimed those resources for themselves. This was a major institutional innovation that led to the spontaneous development of private property rights in the American West. And the American West became a major laboratory for economic analysis of the history and development of property rights (Anderson and Hill, 2004).

As the flow of settlers from Europe increased, so did the value of land in the American West. Consequently, the frontier (theoretically, the line defining the zero marginal value of land) kept moving further and further to the west. As the frontier was pushed westward additional resources became available for settlers. In order for newly acquired resources to yield positive returns, settlers had to develop a set of rules governing access to those resources. In other words, they had to reduce transaction costs. Otherwise the potential gains would have been dissipated among competing claimants. To that end, the settlers in various parts of the American West created social compacts that regulated the right of access to scarce resources for the original group and future newcomers. Those compacts combined the cultural, moral and religious constraints of settlers with the survival requirements of new frontiers. To monitor and enforce those compacts, the settlers elected enforcers such as sheriffs.

The quest for economic efficiency dictated the transformation of social compacts into formal rules. As the number of settlers continued to grow, competition between rival groups for scarce resources (e.g., farmers competing with ranchers) required a stronger enforcer. Also, by providing free information about the standard terms of exchange, formal rules reduced the costs of contracting across various groups of settlers. Finally, common law judges turned out to be much more proficient at interpreting formal rules they repeatedly used than at interpreting the terms and intent of individual contractual agreements. In time, common law judges accepted those rules, and they eventually became the law of the land.

PRIVATE PROPERTY RIGHTS, INCENTIVES AND EXCHANGE

Ever since Adam Smith's *Wealth of Nations*, economics has been regarded as the science of exchange. Voluntary exchange can only take place if individuals' rights to use or dispose of goods that are being exchanged are clearly specified and exclusive. And the terms of exchange depend on the bundle of rights that are being transferred from one person to another. The value of a membership in the local country club depends on whether my children are allowed to use tennis courts.

The right of ownership contains three elements: exclusivity of ownership, transferability of ownership and constitutional guarantees of ownership. Those three elements set private property rights apart from other types of property rights and generate incentives that have efficiency-friendly effects on economic performance.

Exclusivity of ownership means that the owner decides what to do with his asset, captures the benefits of the decision, and bears its cost. Exclusivity of ownership then creates a strong link between one's right to choose how to use one's property and bearing the consequences of that choice. By implication, exclusivity of ownership creates incentives for the owner to move his resources to the highest-value use that he is capable of discovering. The transferability of ownership provides two interrelated efficiency-friendly incentives. Individuals buy and sell assets because they expect to be better off after exchange than before it. Thus, the transfer of ownership is expected to move resources from a lower- to a higher-valued user. Also the transferability of ownership means that the owner has a choice to take the value of his assets in a lump sum or as a flow over the productive life of those assets. An important consequence of this choice, which other types of property rights do not provide, is that individuals can rearrange their portfolios in accordance with their subjective perceptions of what the future holds as well as their attitude toward risk. The constitutional guarantee of ownership eliminates the bias against decisions that have long-term value consequences.

It is a fact that many societies have not adopted private property rights. We also observe all sorts of restrictions on private property. We can also see that societies that are ruled by well-specified and well-enforced property right systems have done better in terms of economic growth than others.[7] Bernhard Heitger (2004) finds that 'estimating the direct relationship between property rights and end-of-period per capita incomes yields a highly significant regressor and indicates that a doubling in the index of property rights more than doubles living standards'. Private property rights then create efficiency-friendly incentives to deal with economic problems of who gets what and who does what.

ECONOMIC EFFICIENCY OF ALTERNATIVE PROPERTY RIGHTS

In addition to private property rights, a number of other institutional arrangements are used to define the right of access to scarce resources. In this section, we briefly compare the efficiency effects of the absence of property rights, the right of ownership, attenuated private property rights and state ownership.

Consider a single tree (or any other good that yields a flow of returns over time). Like all other resources this tree has alternative uses. At any given time, it could be cut and the proceeds from the sale of lumber could be invested in another asset. On the other hand, keeping the tree alive preserves the annual increments in the value of lumber. Two important issues are then (1) when is the most appropriate time to cut a live tree, and (2) what are the incentive effects of alternative property rights on the choice of time to cut the tree?

Suppose a passer-by sees a young tree that nobody owns. The value of lumber in that tree is minimal but positive, and the passer-by might decide against cutting it. Yet it has to occur to him that, if he does not cut the tree, someone else might. The passer-by might also consider keeping the tree alive so that he can cut it at some later date. But the transaction costs of monitoring and protecting his claim (e.g., hiring an armed guard) are likely to be prohibitive relative to the value of lumber in that tree a few years later. On the other hand, the cost of cutting a small tree is low; it takes an axe and a few minutes of labor. So this passer-by (or the next one) will cut it *now* and sell whatever little lumber it contains to a lumberyard. A testable implication is that non-owned assets are overused and underproduced.

Suppose, in contrast, that John owns a tree. Driven by his self-interest, John seeks to maximize his returns from that assert. The issue facing the owner is when is the best time to cut the tree and sell it to the lumberyard. The optimal time for cutting the tree depends on the relationship between the annual increment in the value of lumber in the live tree and the prevailing rate of interest from cutting the tree. As long as the annual increase in the value of lumber in the live tree exceeds the rate of interest, John has incentives to keep the tree alive. Since trees grow at a declining rate, the rate of growth in the value of lumber in John's tree will eventually approach the rate of interest. At that point – neither sooner nor later – he would have incentives to cut the tree, sell the lumber from the felled tree to a lumberyard, and invest the proceeds into another asset.

Trees yield social benefits. They purify the air, beautify landscapes and provide a livelihood and resting places for birds, small animals and insects. Keeping the tree alive has social costs. People use wood for homes, airplanes, cars, furniture and many other products. The more trees we cut, the cheaper those goods will be, and vice versa. An important implication is that cutting a tree does not destroy a resource. It merely changes its use. From the point of view of the community as a whole, the best time to cut the tree is also when the rate of increase in the value of lumber approximates the prevailing rate of interest. The conclusion is that the incentives provided by the right of ownership tend to close the gap between the private and social costs of the allocation of scarce resources among alternative uses. The incentive effects of the right of ownership are consistent with efficient outcomes.

A change in the rate of interest is an important determinant of the allocation of privately owned assets between alternative uses. At a higher rate of interest the owner would cut the tree sooner. That would lower the price of wood and home builders would substitute wood for steel. At a higher rate of interest, a cattleman from Texas would slaughter his yearlings earlier. That would raise the price of aged beef. And at a higher rate of interest a grape grower from California would send more grapes to local markets raising the price of wine.

Most West European countries have enacted laws that attenuate private property rights in privately owned firms. The attenuation of the right of ownership in business firms raises the costs of running business firms. And higher costs of running business firms leads to less demand for workers and more unemployment. Good examples are labor laws in France (and most other countries in Western Europe) and codetermination in Germany. The latter is an experiment in the enhancement of industrial policy. The former is a vehicle for wealth redistribution via political process.

Codetermination means labor participation in the management of business firms. The major feature of codetermination in Germany is that workers are represented on the board of directors and are thus given an active role in running business firms. Codetermination has not arisen voluntarily. It is mandated by law. That is in itself the best evidence of the economic inefficiency of codetermination.

Codetermination forces investors to share the responsibility for business decisions with people whose assets are not firm-specific. And sharing the responsibility for business decisions creates a conflict of interest between investors and employees.[8] The conflict arises from two simple facts. First, business decisions impose different risks on investors and employees. If the firm is successful in making profits, the gains will be shared by both groups, depending on the outcome of the bargaining process. If the firm goes bankrupt, shareholders will lose the full value of wealth invested in the company, while employees will lose only the flow of income while looking for another job. And if they were paid no more than the opportunity cost, their losses are bound to be minimal.

The second source of conflict between investors and employees arises from differences in their respective time horizons. The workers' time horizon is limited to their expected employment by the firm, since they capture the benefits only while working for the firm. On the other hand, owners/investors face no time limit, for they can always cash in the present value of the future expected returns on their investment. Such differences in time horizon have consequences. For example, consider two investment alternatives of equal cost. The expected present value of one alternative is $1000 while the other yields only $750 at the going rate of interest. However, if the returns from the first alternative are expected over a period of 20 years and those of the second over only five years, employees have incentives to make business decisions that promise larger cash flows in the short run (and thus more juice to share to the benefit of the current workers), rather than policies that maximize the firm's present value.

The attenuation of private property rights then changes the returns to privately owned assets, increasing the transaction costs of identifying, negotiating and exploiting the most beneficial exchange opportunities. Most important, the attenuation of private property rights tends to increase the rate of interest over and above what it would have been in a regime of stable and credible property rights. Going back to our example, the equality between the rate of increase in the value of lumber in the live tree and the observed market rate of interest would then occur earlier than under a regime of credible private property rights. And the tree would then be cut too early.

Under a regime of state ownership, only the top political leaders and the top bureaucrats have (often conflicting) claims on productive assets. Decision makers in government have rather weak incentives to relate the rate of growth in the value of lumber in the live tree to the going rate of interest. Political enhancement plays a more important role. Of course, it may happen that trees are cut when the rate of growth in the value of their lumber actually approaches the rate of interest. In fact, economic analysis cannot predict when the government will cut its trees. There are examples of forests that have been devastated to provide governments with cash. There are also many examples in which trees have not been cut because the government was influenced by those who consider the conservation of wildlife a superior good. The latter argue that many individuals have wrong ideas about the most valuable use for those resources. As Armen Alchian likes to say, such an argument is simply an assertion that individuals they disagree with should be denied the right to satisfy their preferences in open markets.

NOTES

1. The term 'group' is important, for in ancient Rome rights to use the land were not attributed to the individual, but to the members of clans. This clearly favored the aristocracy, which was structured in *gentes*, to the detriment of the plebeians, who were a network of independent families.
2. Rome was founded as a trading post. In particular it consisted of rocky ground on the hills (suitable for defensive purposes) and marshes on the plain. Agriculture was thus far from attractive.
3. See also Zuccotti (2003), who points out that the privatization of the *ager publicus* led to the weakening of the *gens*-based aristocracy and thus to deep changes in the political structure of the state. Although the details of the privatization process cannot be ascertained, the notion of private property had already replaced that of clan property at the time of the XII Tables (440s BC) and was already accomplished when political discrimination between patricians and plebeians was removed (*Lex Licinia Sextia*, 367 BC).
4. To be precise, according to the Bible, Adam and Eve were supposed to grow their food. However, there are two important elements that made Adam and Eve in the Garden of Eden different from us. Whatever they did in order to grow their food, their work was not associated with labor and fatigue. The acquisition of knowledge and the satisfaction of unmet needs were not an issue.
5. See Alexander (2003, pp. 101–44).
6. From article 42 of the Italian Constitution (unoffocial translation): 'Private property is accepted and guaranteed by the law, which determines how it can be acquired, how and within which limits it can be enjoyed, so as to ensure its social function and free access by everybody.'
7. This reference is to sustainable growth. One should rule out cases where growth is made temporarily possible by government measures such as direct public investement, incentives (e.g., tax breaks) to invest and massive foreign debt. All these and similar cases interfere with the allocation of resources based on voluntary exchange between individuals and have no positive long-run benefits.
8. Instead of being a free exchange of ideas, thoughts and judgments about serving the interest of investors, discussions in the board room are a sort of bargaining process between two sides, one acting to advance the interests of the owners of the company, one striving to acquire privileges for the labor force. Of course, the problem also extends to the relationship between the management and the board. See M. Paul, 'Germany's Requiring of Workers on Boards Causes Many Problems', *Wall Street Journal*, 10 December 1979.

REFERENCES

Alexander, G. (2003), 'Property as a fundamental constitutional right? The German example', *Cornell Law Review*, **88**(3), 101–44.

Anderson, T. and P. Hill (2004), *The Not So Wild, Wild West,* Palo Alto: Stanford University Press.

Anderson, T. and D. Leal (2001), *Free Market Environmentalism*, New York: Palgrave.

Bauer, P. (1991), *The Development Frontier*, London: Harvester Wheatsheaf.

Buchanan, J. (1979), *What Should Economists Do?*, Indianapolis: Liberty Press.

Buchanan, J. and C. Stubblebine (1962), 'Externality', *Economica*, **29**, 371–84.

De Jasay, A. (1998), 'Prisoners' dilemma and the theory of the state', in Peter Newman (ed.), *The New Palgrave Dictionary of Economics and the Law*, London: Macmillan, pp. 95–103.

Epstein, R. (1994), 'On the optimal mix of private and common property', *Social Philosophy and Policy*, **1**(2), 17–41.

Fisher, I. (1916), Elementary *Principles of Economics*, New York: Macmillan.

Heitger, B (2004), 'Property rights and the wealth of nations: a cross-country study', *Cato Journal*, **23**(4), 381–402.

Liggio, L. and A. Chafuen (2004), 'Cultural and religious foundations of private property', in Enrico Colombatto (ed.), *The Elgar Companion to the Economics of Property Rights,* Cheltenham, UK and Northampton, MA, USA: Edward Elgar, pp. 3–47.

Maddison, A. (1995), *Monitoring the World Economy 1820–1992*, Paris: OECD Development Centre.

North, Douglass (1988), 'Institutions, economic growth, and freedom: a historical introduction', in M. Walker (ed.), *Freedom, Democracy and Economic Welfare*, Vancouver: Fraser Institute, pp. 14–19.

North, D. and B. Weingast (1989), 'Constitutions and commitment: the evolution of institutions governing public choice in seventeenth-century England', *Journal of Economic History*, **49**(4), 803–32.

Zuccotti, Ferdinando (2003), 'I glittodonti del diritto romano. Alcune ipotesi sulle strutture dell'arcaico ordinamento quiritario', *Rivista di Diritto Romano*, **III**, 389–421.

8. Capitalism, economic freedom and performance

A growing body of literature supports the premise that formal and informal institutions affect economic performance, and empirical evidence supports it as well. Given that premise, linking capitalism with economic performance are incentives that the institutions of capitalism generate and the effects of those incentives on transaction costs. And this linkage between capitalism and economic performance has produced economic results that no other institutions and systems have been able to duplicate. A few simple observations suffice to confirm this statement.

The capitalist West has done much better than the rest, while Hong Kong and Singapore have become the economic showcases for the rest of the world. The economy of China started growing as soon as its leaders replaced the little red book with the bottom line. Many countries in East Asia and Africa gained independence from colonial regimes at various times in the 1950s and 1960s. At that time those two regions were at about the same level of economic underdevelopment. Just a few decades after gaining independence East Asia became a model of economic success, while Africa stagnated.[1] A plausible explanation for observed differences in economic growth between those two regions is that East Asian societies found a way to integrate their informal rules with the institutions of capitalism, while most African countries opted for 'their own way' to socialism.

It is also observable that, at the turn of the twenty-first century, Anglo-American capitalism, which is much closer to the roots of classical liberalism, has been doing better than the Continental capitalism. Richard Rahn (2 January 2006) described the economic situation in Western Europe in the early 2000s as follows: 'Europe has not yet suffered from bird flu, but it suffers from an even more debilitating economic flu: excessive government dependency. That dependency is sapping both its economic vitality and its spirit and has grown most acute in the core of Europe: Germany, France and Italy.'

The Index of Economic Freedom, published jointly by the Heritage Foundation and the *Wall Street Journal* and the Economic Freedom of the World Index published by the Fraser Institute confirm observations about economic results of Anglo-American and Continental capitalism. To measure economic freedom, both indexes use categories that are consistent with the institutions and policies of classical capitalism.[2] The Fraser Institute, the Heritage Foundation and the *Wall Street Journal* provide detailed explanations about the methodology they use in compiling their respective indexes. It is important to note that both indexes are about economic freedom only. Political and civil freedoms are not included in either of these two indexes.

Like all indexes, the two indexes of economic freedom have technical limitations and methodological problems. However, they are the best we have. Moreover, they have passed the test of time. Scholars use both indexes in their research. Investors are paying close attention to the ranking of countries in terms of economic freedoms. Foreign embassies call to complain about the rankings of their respective countries. De Haan and Sturm (2000) tested the Fraser Index and found that greater economic freedom fosters economic growth, but that the level of economic freedom is not related to growth. Stocker (2005) got similar results. He found (p. 589) that 'increases in economic freedom are associated with higher equity returns [statistically significant at the 99 per cent confidence level] while the absolute level of beginning and ending economic freedom do not affect equity returns'.

Both indexes confirm that the freer a country is the better is its economic performance over a long period of time. James Gwartney wrote (2003, p. 3): 'The maintenance over a lengthy period of time of institutions and policies consistent with economic freedom is a major determinant of cross-country differences in per capita GDP ... cross-country differences in the mean rating during 1980–2000 explain 63.2 percent of the cross-country variations in 2000 per capita GDP.' Importantly, both indexes show that, with some delays and bumps, there has been a definite worldwide trend toward more economic freedom.

For consistency, I use the Index of Economic Freedom published by the Heritage Foundation and the *Wall Street Journal* (hereafter: *Index*). Until 2006, the Index classified all countries into four broad categories of economic freedom: *free* (1–1.99), *mostly free* (2.00–2.99), *mostly unfree* (3.00–3.99) and *repressed* (4.00 or higher). The highest ranking Western country in the 2006 Index was Ireland with the overall score of 1.58. The highest ranking countries in the world were Hong Kong and Singapore, with the scores of 1.28 and 1.56, respectively.

The Index also shows that, over the past ten years, there has been a trend toward more economic freedom. The median score for all countries (always around 160) improved from 3.23 in 1997 to 3.04 in 2006. This meant that in 2006 close to one-half of 161 countries were close to being 'mostly free' (classification of 2.99). The 2006 Index also divided all countries into five groups based on their improvements in economic freedom between 1997 and 2006. The average growth rates in per capita income were then computed for each of those five groups (ibid., p. 3). The results showed that countries which improved their economic freedom most experienced the highest average economic growth of income per capita (4.06 percent, 3.0 percent, 1.4 percent, 1.3 percent and 1.5 percent, respectively).

As I said earlier, the categories used by the Index to measure economic freedom are consistent with the institutions and policies of capitalism and, consequently, with economic efficiency. Thus to say that a country has increased its score of economic freedom is the same as saying that the country has come closer to the concept of classical capitalism, which is the score of one. Mary O'Grady wrote in the *Wall Street Journal* (16 January 2007) that 'the 2007 Index finds that economically free countries enjoy significantly greater prosperity than those burdened by heavy government intervention'.

Let us now make use of the Index to compare the effects of common law and civil codes on economic freedom in capitalist countries.

The Period from 1996–2006

The analysis in Chapters 3–7 suggests that, relative to civil codes, the incentive effects of common law are more efficiency-friendly. The Index should then be expected to show that common law countries have lower scores (i.e., that they are freer) than civil law states. To test this proposition, Western capitalist countries (in the cultural rather than geographical sense) are separated into two groups. The first group consists of countries in which common law is a dominant legal system. Those are the United States, England, Ireland, Australia, Canada and New Zealand. Singapore and Hong Kong are left out because it is not clear whether they are part of Western civilization. The second group of countries includes all Western countries that use civil law. Those countries are Portugal, Spain, France, Luxembourg, Germany, Belgium, Holland, Italy, Switzerland, Austria, Sweden and Denmark. Left out are Greece, which was dominated by the Ottoman Empire for centuries, Finland, which has somehow remained between the West and the East, and Norway, which uses both common law and civil law.

Table 8.1 shows the average scores for those two groups of countries in 1996 and 2006. It appears that, relative to civil law, common law has been more protective of the institutions of capitalism. In 2006, the average score for civil law countries remained almost in the *mostly free* category (2.00–2.99), while common law countries were firmly in the *free* category.

Table 8.2 reduces the comparison between civil law and common law countries to four major capitalist states representing the Continental and Anglo-American capitalism: France, Germany, England and the United States. The comparison makes an even stronger case for common law. While neither legal system has been able to tame the state (that is, to get close to the score of one), economic freedoms in Anglo-American capitalism have remained much stronger.

Table 8.1 Economic freedom in common law and civil law countries

Legal tradition	Type of capitalism	Score, 2006	Score, 1996
Common law	Anglo-American	1.78	2.00
Civil law	Continental	1.98	2.30

Source: Miles et al. (2006). The scale is 1 to 5, with 1 representing the greatest economic freedom.

Table 8.2 Economic freedom in major capitalist countries

Legal tradition	Type of capitalism	Score, 2006	Score, 1996
Common Law	Anglo-American	1.79	1.94
Civil Law	Continental	2.23	2.33

Source: Miles et al. (2006).

Still another important test involves the protective effects of common law and civil law on the rule of law. Some of the categories that comprise the Index are more closely related to the rule of law than others. For example, scores for property rights reflect the credibility of the right of ownership while black market activities are a major consequence of the attenuation of the freedom of exchange. On the other hand, scores on banking and finance, and on monetary policy, do not necessarily contain the same message about the strength of the rule of law (the former USSR was fiscally very tight). Moreover, a poor score on the fiscal burden of government might reflect expenditures necessary to enhance national security. For example, the United States and the United Kingdom expenditures for national defense during the Cold War years were bound to have a negative impact on their scores for economic freedom, yet at the same time those expenditures helped to protect the private-property, free-market economies of Western Europe.

The issue, then, is to identify those categories in the Index that are closely tied to the rule of law. I conjecture that the following three categories bear on the rule of law: private property rights, government regulations and the black market. The importance of property rights is self-evident. A poor score for government regulations suggests considerable interference with efficiency-friendly voluntary interactions. Black market activities are both normal and predictable responses to constraints on the freedom of contract, an important element of the rule of law.

Tables 8.3 and 8.4 include the same countries as Tables 8.1 and 8.2, respectively, but with one critical difference: average scores in Tables 8.3 and 8.4 are

Table 8.3   The rule of law and economic freedom

Legal tradition	Type of capitalism	Score, 2006	Score, 1996
Common Law	Anglo-American	1.39	1.55
Civil law	Continental	1.83	1.80

Source: Miles et al. (2006).

Table 8.4   The rule of law and economic freedom in major capitalist countries

Legal tradition	Type of capitalism	Score, 2006	Score, 1996
Common law	Anglo-American	1.41	1.33
Civil law	Continental	2.08	1.66

Source: Miles et al. (2006).

based only on property rights, black markets and government regulations; that is, on the three categories that are arguably closely tied to the rule of law.

Table 8.3 shows that common law protects the rule of law better than does civil law. Table 8.4 suggests that, between 1996 and 2006, the rule of law has grown worse in all four major capitalist countries. One is tempted to say that, while the rest are trying to move on, the four dinosaurs are running out of steam.

The Effects of Recent Changes in the Index of Economic Freedom

The Heritage Foundation and the *Wall Street Journal* made three important changes in the 2007 Index. The method of grading countries changed from a scale of 1 to 5, where the score of 1 was the best, to a scale of 1 to 100 with the score of 100 being the best. The 2007 Index also increased the number of categories of economic freedom from four to five. Those categories are *free* (80–100), *mostly free* (70–79.9), moderately free (60–69.9), mostly unfree (50–59.9) and *repressed* (0–49.9).

The most important change made in the 2007 Index was the introduction of two new categories for evaluating economic freedom. Business Freedom replaced Regulations, and Labor Freedom replaced Wages and Prices; Wages and Prices are now combined with Monetary Freedom. Business Freedom is still about regulations, but it emphasizes regulations affecting the transaction costs of entrepreneurship, including the costs of opening and closing businesses. Labor Freedom evaluates institutional constraints and policy restrictions on the working of the labor market, such as the freedom to hire and fire workers, control of working hours, and the minimum wage.

The Heritage Foundation and the *Wall Street Journal* did provide the method for reconciling information from the period 1996–2006 with changes in 2007. It might be both interesting and important to discover how and to what extent new changes in the Index affect the results in Tables 8.1 and 8.2.

In the old Index, scores of 1–1.9 classified countries as *free*. Converting the new classification of free countries (80–100) into the old one, we get scores of 1–1.8 (remembering that the score of one is the best). The classification of the group of freest countries is now slightly more rigorous, and this change in the classification of the freest countries did make a difference in the 2007 Index. It classifies only seven countries as *free* countries (Hong Kong, Singapore, Australia, the United States, New Zealand, United Kingdom and Ireland). All seven free countries are also common law countries. Luxembourg, Iceland, Estonia and Denmark moved back to the *mostly free* category.

Tables 8.5 and 8.6 include the same countries as Tables 8.1 and 8.2. The third column shows the average scores in 2007, based on the new scale of 1–100. Column four converts the new scores into the old ones. We observe no major difference between the results for 2007 and the old system.

While the conversion of the old into the new scale is technically simple, the converted numbers may not be fully comparable because of changes in the categories for measuring freedom. For that reason, no attempt is made to compare information contained in Tables 8.3 and 8.4 with data in 2007.

It is arguable then, empirically as well as analytically, that the combination of formal and informal institutions in the West created an economic system, that

Table 8.5   Economic freedom in common law and civil law countries

Legal tradition	Type of capitalism	Score, 2007	Harmonized score
Common law	Anglo-American	81.30	1.75
Civil law	Continental	72.66	2.1

Table 8.6   Economic freedom in major capitalist countries

Legal tradition	Type of capitalism	Score, 2007	Harmonized score
Common Law	Anglo-American	81.76	1.6
Civil Law	Continental	69.81	2.2

has not only elevated the average individual above a subsistence standard of living but sustained continuous per capita economic growth.

PERFORMANCE OF BUSINESS FIRMS AND THE CHOICE OF LEGAL SYSTEM

In capitalist countries we observe all sorts of business organizations such as corporations, single proprietorships, producers' cooperatives, labor cooperatives, associations, not-for-profit firms, partnerships, and other types of teamwork. All those types of firms have been organized voluntarily and have survived competition from other types of business organizations; that is, they have passed the efficiency test. Among all those different types of business forms, the corporate firm stands out as the most productive method for organizing production. Questions are: what are the advantages of the corporate firm over other types of private-ownership enterprises? Does the efficiency of corporate firms depend on the choice of legal system?

The advantage, which sets the corporation apart from other types of business firms, derives from the anonymous alienability of shares. Anonymity is made possible by limited liability. Individual owners of the firm (shareholders) need not care who other owners are. This enables shareholders to buy and sell shares without requiring the approval of other owners of the firm. That translates into a substantial reduction in the transaction costs of raising large amounts of capital and that is why the modern corporation is the most effective method of *voluntarily* gathering large amounts of capital for long-lived ventures.

However, the ability of the corporate firm to attract a large number of buyers depends on the strong protection of investors. The protection of investors presupposes the freedom of contract and credible property rights. The former reduces the transaction costs of entry and exit from business, while the latter protects shareholders' wealth from redistribution in political markets. Together, the freedom of contract and private property rights encourage the expansion of trade and technological innovation. Moreover, the strong protection of investors creates strong incentives for small savers to become shareholders. The dispersion of shareholding should then correlate with the protection of shareholders. The dispersion of shareholding is important because it has many economic benefits. Let us mention a few.

The dispersion of shareholding means that investors, small and large, can diversify their portfolios and avoid firm-specific risk. Thus individuals have incentives to invest in risky ventures thanks to the ability to mitigate those risks through diversification (Macey,1998). The dispersion of shareholding then encourages innovations, risk taking and bearing the consequences of one's decision. The dispersion of ownership contributes to the development of the middle class with significant and diversifiable stakes in the free-market, private-property economy.

Aside from the tiny fraction of corporate activists, all that shareholders want is the highest possible value for their shares. By selling or threatening to sell their shares in transparent financial markets, shareholders lower the transaction costs of replacing management. Hence corporate managers have strong incentives to pursue shareholders' interests.

A growing body of literature (e.g., Demsetz and Lehn, 1985; La Porta et al., 1999; Chhibber and Majumdar, 1999; Roe, 2000; Manne, 2005; Mueller, 2005) shows that common law protects shareholders better than do statutory laws. Predictably, empirical evidence shows that the dispersion of shareholding is much greater in the United States than in Western Europe, where large families, a few large shareholders and financial institutions like banks own shares. And differences in the dispersion of shareholding, which reflect the attenuation of private property rights, have economic consequences. In a major and well-documented study, Klaus Gugler, Dennis Mueller and Burcin Yurtoglu (2004, p.589) summarized their findings as follows:

> We show that the origin of a country's legal system proves to be the most important determinant of investment performance. Companies in countries with a legal system of English origin earn returns on investment that are at least as large as their costs of capital. Companies in all countries with civil-law systems earn on average returns on investment below their costs of capital. Furthermore, differences in investment performance that are related to a country's legal system dominate differences that are related to ownership structure.

Interestingly, Katharina Pistor (2000) found that the corporate laws developed in various parts of the former Soviet bloc resemble those of the countries offering legal assistance (French, German USAID, etc). She observes that 'the strong similarities of laws that were influenced by identifiable groups of foreign advisors suggest that the contents of legal rules ... were strongly influenced by the group of advisors that dominated in a given country' (p.27). A suggestion for future research is to look into differences in investment performance of those countries.

NOTES

1. See a very instructive piece by Keith Richburg, 'Why is Black Africa overwhelmed while East Asia overcomes?', *International Herald Tribune*, 14 July 1992, pp. 1 and 6.
2. The Fraser Index uses the following factors, which are then broken down into subcategories, to rank countries in terms of economic freedom: size of government, economic structure and use of markets, monetary policy and inflation, freedom to use alternative currencies, credibility and stability of property rights, free trade and freedom of exchange in capital markets. Until 2006, the Heritage Foundation and the *Wall Street Journal* used the following factors, also

broken down into subcategories: fiscal burden of government, government intervention in the economy, monetary policy, capital flows and foreign investments, banking and finance, wages and prices, property rights, government regulation, and black market. As of 2007, the Index of Economic Freedom uses the following 10 factors: business freedom, trade freedom, fiscal freedom, freedom from government, monetary freedom, investment freedom, financial freedom, property rights, freedom from corruption and labor freedom.

REFERENCES

Chhibber, P. and S. Majumdar (1999), 'Foreign ownership and profitability: property rights, control, and the performance of firms in Indian industry', *Journal of Law and Economics*, **17**(10), 209–38.

De Haan, J. and J. Sturm (2000), 'On the relationship between economic freedom and economic growth', *European Journal of Political Economy*, **16**(2), 215–41.

Demsetz, H. and K. Lehn (1985), 'The structure of corporate ownership: causes and consequences', *Journal of Political Economy*, **93**(6), 1155–77.

Gwartney, J. (2003), 'What have we learned from the measurement of economic freedom?', paper presented at the conference on *The Legacy of Milton and Rose Friedman's Free to Choose: Economic Liberalism at the Turn of the 21st Century*, Federal Reserve Bank of Dallas.

Kane, T., K. Holmes and M. O'Grady, (eds) (2007), *Index of Economic Freedom*, Washington, D.C.: Heritage Foundation and *Wall Street Journal*.

La Porta, R., F. Lopez-De-Silanes and A. Shleifer (1999), 'Corporate ownership around the world', *Journal of Finance*, **54**(2), 471–513.

Macey, J. (1998), 'Gli Stati Uniti: Un Paese Senze Legge', Working Paper No. 2, International Centre for Economic Research, Turin.

Manne, H. (2005), 'Insider trading: Hayek, virtual markets and the dog that did not bark', *Journal of Corporation Law*, **31**(1), 167–85.

Miles, M., K. Holmes and M. O'Grady (eds) (2006), *Index of Economic Freedom*, Washington, D.C.: Heritage Foundation and *Wall Street Journal*.

Mueller, D. (2005), 'The economics and politics of corporate governance in the European Union', *Law Working Paper No. 37/2005*, European Corporate Governance Institute, pp. 1–41.

Pistor, K (2000), 'Patterns of legal change: shareholder and creditor rights in transition economies', *Working Paper* No. 49, European Bank for Reconstruction and Development, Basel.

Roe, Mark J. (2000), 'Political foundations for separating ownership from control', *Stanford Law Review*, **53** (December), 1–16.

Stocker, M. (2005), 'Equity returns and economic freedom', *Cato Journal*, **25**(3), Fall, 583–94.

9. The rule of law and capitalism: an overview

The economic efficiency of the use of resources is judged by the openness of the process through which voluntary interactions are carried out. Thus, a set of institutions that offers greater incentives for voluntary interactions is more efficient than another set of institutions that provides weaker incentives for free exchange. An Italian's freedom to choose to spend 1000 euros on fast cars represents a more efficient use of resources than using the strong-hand-of-the-state to force him (via tax or some other 'incentives') to invest the same 1000 euros in a project that promises 10 percent growth. That is so because the latter interferes both with the Italian's freedom to pursue his own ends and with scarcity prices that can only be established via voluntary interactions.

The incentive effects of open market competition and the freedom of choice are efficiency-friendly. Competition reduces the transaction costs of exchange by conglomerating information about exchange opportunities and the terms of exchange for all the various goods. Freedom of choice allows individuals to exploit those exchange opportunities in accordance with their subjectively determined cost/benefit ratios. Observed (market) prices are the outcome of those voluntary human interactions.[1] If individuals had complete information about all exchange opportunities and if information were equally available to all individuals, observed prices would be true scarcity prices.

Individuals have limited abilities to predict the future, while their subjective perceptions of reality and evaluations of the same set of exchange opportunities differ from one person to another. Thus we have no way of knowing how large or small the gap might be between observed prices and true scarcity prices at any given time. The best we can do is to search for institutions that create incentives for interacting individuals to engage in behavior that narrows the gap between observed and scarcity prices. That is why the economic efficiency of the use of resources is impaired by outside interferences with the process through which voluntary interactions are carried out.

Through their TV series *The Freedom to Choose*, Milton and Rose Friedman have made the free-market, private-property economy better understood by the median voter than have the writings of all other free-market economists combined. And better understanding of economic freedoms by the median voter could and, in fact did, lead to better protection of the rule of law. Good examples are the years of Ronald Reagan and Margaret Thatcher in the 1980s, and the 1996 welfare reform in the United States.

On the other hand, the technobureaucratic approach that is common to Continental capitalism can be summarized as follows: scholars prepare a set of policies that promise to yield the desired outcome, then the observed results of those policies diverge from policy makers' expectations. To fix the problem the government has to make additional policies. Those policies increase the interference with the freedom of individuals to make their own choices, and that interference increases the gap between what the state has compelled people to do and what they would otherwise have done. Ronald Coase argued that, if all those desired blackboard models were carried out, the allocation of resources would indeed be optimal. However, he said (1988, p. 179): 'My point is that such policies are the stuff that dreams are made of. In my youth it was said that what was silly to be said may be sung. In modern economics it may be put into mathematics.' The four basic institutions embodied in the rule of law (private property rights, the constitution, the law of contract, and an independent judiciary) protect individuals from such interference with their freedom to choose. And in so doing those institutions increase the extent of exchange.

The costs of economic efficiency or, conversely, the costs of protecting private property rights and the freedom of choice, rise as the world gets more complex. This increase in the costs of protecting economic freedoms eventually outstrips the ability of informal rules to safeguard open market competition and the freedom of choice. At that point, informal rules and arrangements are institutionalized, as happened in England in the early seventeenth century, when common law began replacing the law merchant.

The incentive effects of the heritage of Greece and Rome and the nuclear family played a key role in influencing the path of institutional restructuring in the West. The heritage of Greece justified the replacement of the revealed truth with inquisitive reasoning, which became a springboard for the development of science. Pope Gregory I (590–604) initiated the process that eventually replaced the extended family with the nuclear family and, arguably, accelerated the rise of individualism (Deepak, 1998, p. 83). By encouraging the concept of a polity consisting of natural equals, the nuclear family in the West has created incentives for bonding among individuals across family lines. In short, the rise of the nuclear family explains some critical differences between the culture of individualism in the West and the culture of collectivism elsewhere.[2]

This process of institutionalizing classical liberalism into capitalism moved along different paths in England and on the Continent. In seventeenth-century England, common law provided the legal framework for classical liberalism and methodological individualism.[3] The legal systems of the United States, Canada, Ireland, Australian and New Zealand evolved from English common law, while civil codes dominated the development of formal rules in Western

Europe.[4] The common law and civil code then provided the legal foundations for the rule of law, an essential cornerstone of the Anglo-American and Continental capitalism.

Table 9.1 summarizes three major differences between Anglo-American and Continental capitalism. Those differences relate to the perceived nature of capitalism, the role of the state, and the protection of the freedom of choice and private property rights.

Table 9.1   Anglo-American and continental capitalism: major characteristics

Anglo-American capitalism	Continental capitalism
The system is self-generating, self-correcting and self-regulating	The state must take care of market failures and other problems
The government is a predator which the rule of law is to tame	The government is a partner in the economic game
The system is about the freedom of choice and private property rights	The system superimposes social justice over the freedom of choice

This idealized concept of the rule of law (as defined by Leoni and Hayek) probably never existed. However, it is a useful yardstick against which we can evaluate the prevailing institutions in any country as well as the consistency of proposed institutional reforms with the rule of law. To play down the importance of the rule of law just because it has been compromised would be a grave mistake. For such a decision would deprive us of an important standard against which we can evaluate social changes in terms of their effects on open market competition and individual liberty. That is so because, relative to various blackboard models and utopian concepts of a good society, the four basic institutions that the rule of law embodies, however watered down they might be, do exist as positive formal laws in the West. Moreover, those institutions – that is, private property rights, the law of contracts, an independent judiciary and a constitution – have been integrated into the Western institutional landscape over a long time. And so has the concept of limited government relative to the philosophically preferred concept of a minimal state. Limited government refers to the number of functions the rule of law assigns to the state, a good example being the tenth amendment to the United States Constitution. A minimal state is about the size of the state apparatus.

The implementation of the rule of law does not require institutional reforms because its institutions are firmly entrenched in Western legal tradition. It is less costly to enforce existing institutions that have proved their worth than to enact untested ones. Thus the rule of law and a limited state are the lowest cost protections we have against collectivism, socialism, fascism and other utopian experiments with human beings. Walter Williams wrote (1994, p. 24): 'Fascism, communism and socialism are kindred forms of collectivism whose survival critically depends upon undermining of private property rights, rule of law, limited government and other institutions. Collectivists everywhere disdain the rule of law, traditions and the market place in favor of the direct pursuit of intended outcomes.'

TWO LEGAL SYSTEMS AND THEIR INCENTIVES

Formal rules are a policy variable. Hence it matters who the law makers are and what their incentives are. That is so because the process of making formal rules affects both the behavior of individuals and economic performance. And it is the process of law making that makes the two legal traditions diverge from each other. In the Anglo-American common law tradition, formal rules are generalized from specific decisions entered by common law judges. The major source of those decisions is precedent. And the major source of precedent is tradition, customs and, in general, informal institutions (Manne, 1997). Richard Posner explained the production of precedents as follows (2003, pp. 553–54):

> When a case is decided, the decision is thereafter a precedent, i.e. a reason for deciding a similar case the same way. While a single precedent is a fragile thing ... an accumulation of precedents dealing with the same question may create a rule of law having the same force as an explicit statutory rule ... The body of precedents in an area of law is a stock of capital goods that yields services over many years to potential disputants in the form of information about legal obligations ... The capital stock of precedents is the joint product of the lawyers and judges engaged in the argument and decision, respectively, of cases, mainly appellate cases ... As old precedents reach obsolescence, eventually ceasing to be a part of the usable stock of precedents, new ones are added to the stock through litigation.

In the Continental tradition, precedents and informal institution have only indirect bearing. Formal rules are written by experts, debated by groups of citizens, and enacted by legislators. Relative to the Anglo-American tradition, where changes in formal rules are incremental, the Continental tradition gives the political elite more room for discrete changes in laws and regulations.[5]

Those differences in the process of making rules create different incentives for the rule makers in the two legal systems. Common law judges, especially in the appellate courts where most precedents are made, have little if any contact with the public at large. It is relatively difficult for outside groups to find a legal way to seek favors from common law judges. Bad laws are usually due to ignorance on the part of common law judges and/or to the imposition of their personal convictions; both of those causes of bad laws are reversible by higher courts. The story is different for the makers of formal rules in civil law countries; that is, for legislators. Their careers as politicians depend on identifying and going along with a majoritarian view on various issues. Their incentives to follow precedents and tradition are slim.[6] It is arguably easier for various organizations and rent-seeking coalitions to influence legislators than judges.

An implication is that the process of law making in common law and civil code countries produces, or can be expected to produce, different results. In common law countries, formal rules grow spontaneously from within the system in response to changes in the requirements of the game. Those adjustments in formal rules reduce the transaction costs of exploiting new exchange opportunities and, in doing so, move resources to higher-valued uses. Formal rules in civil code countries are also made in response to changes in the economic conditions of life. However, legislators in Western Europe also have incentives and discretionary power to enact formal rules that promise to push human interactions towards the results desired by a majority of voters, the median voter, rent seeking groups, or all of these. Those formal rules force the game to adjust to new rules. The bottom line is that the incentive effects of common law are more protective of economic efficiency. Here is some evidence in support of this conclusion.

The owner of a building in the United States is free to choose to convert his apartment building into a parking garage. His freedom of choice is consistent with the right of ownership, a basic institution of the rule of law. The owner of an apartment building in Germany has to consider the welfare effects of his action on tenants. In general, apartment owners in Germany, Italy, France and most West European countries cannot simply choose to give a 'vacate-the-apartment' notice to their respective tenants. The resulting attenuation of private property rights interferes with the freedom of choice and raises the costs of ownership.[7]

The right of an employer to fire employees is an important right. It renders the cost of hiring a worker per unit of time equal to the contractual payment (i.e., wage, fringe benefits and taxes) over the same period of time. That is the situation in the United States and in common law countries in general. However, if a worker cannot be fired at will, as is the case in France, Germany and most civil code countries in Europe, the cost of hiring that worker would be the present value of all future costs while that worker is on the firm's payroll; and those costs are much higher than the total wage cost per unit of time. Predictably, rates of unemployment are usually higher in Germany and France than in the United States. The costs of 'caring' for already employed workers are borne by all other workers, and especially by new entrants into the labor force.

Within the framework of Anglo-American capitalism, those who own resources have a constitutional right to decide what type of business organization they want to form. Indeed, we observe a vast number of different types of organizations such as corporations, cooperatives, partnerships, private proprietorships, employee-owned firms and so on. All those types of voluntary organizations have to survive competition from other types of business firms; that is, they continuously have to pass the market test. Not so in Germany and other civil code countries in Western Europe. German law mandates that the board of directors (supervisory council in German terminology) of business firms employing more than 2000 people must have an equal number of directors representing the shareholders and the employees. In smaller firms, one third of the directors must be appointed by the employees (or their union). The fact that the state has to mandate codetermination and protect it from competition by other types of business firms is the best evidence that this transfer of property rights from those who own resources to those whom they employ is both involuntary and inefficient.[8] Jensen and Meckling (1979, pp. 472–73) captured the essence of this weakening of private property rights as follows:

> Indeed, labor can start, and in rare cases has started firms of its own. Moreover, firms are free to write any kind of contracts they wish with their employees. If they choose to, they can offer no-dismissal no lay-off contracts (tenure at universities). If they choose to, they can establish worker councils and agree not to change production methods without worker approval. Moreover, employers would establish such practices if the benefits exceeded the costs. Furthermore, if laborers value the security and 'self-realization' which such participatory arrangements afford them at more than their costs to the employer, they are in a position to offer voluntary changes which it will pay the employer to take. ... Since those arrangements are [rarely] observed, we infer that workers do not value the security, management participation, etc. at more than the cost of providing them.

It is clear that the history of mankind is the endless evolution of formal and informal rules. Critical questions to be asked in Part III of this book are 'Why has Anglo-American capitalism been more successful than Continental capitalism in maintaining as well as developing efficiency-friendly institutions? What is preventing non-capitalist countries from duplicating the institutions of capitalism?'

NOTES

1. These prices are not givens. They change with changes in knowledge, preferences and the supply of resources.
2. I am grateful to J. Buchanan for a long letter on this issue.
3. As of this writing, though, all UK courts are increasingly subject to EU laws. While nominally Roman-derived, EU laws are all about regulation and direction – not about refining rules of just conduct between citizens. In short, EU law is substantively about the European Commission commanding its provincial entities – the national courts. The same applies to Ireland, another

common law country that has to accept the cession of a degree of sovereignty and the subordination of national law to European law. I owe this point to Peter Clarke from the Institute of Economic Affairs in London.
4. The term 'Western Europe' is not meant as a geographical term. It is used in a cultural context and includes all parts of the former Austro-Hungarian Empire and the Baltic states.
5. The difference between common law and civil code countries is not black and white. The former do rely on statutes and the latter do pay attention to previous courts' decisions. The difference lies in the relative importance of the two methods of making formal rules.
6. Enrico Colombatto argues that, in civil law countries, precedent is becoming more and more important in many public administration cases, where the judge can interpret the law as he or she likes but is under pressure to justify differences with respect to previous similar cases.
7. This does not mean that civil law is undesirable. It could be a consequence of the political system in which the preference of a majority for limitation of choice at the expense of economic efficiency overrides the rights of individuals to seek voluntary contractual arrangements consistent with their own ends, given other people's right to do likewise.
8. 650 firms in Germany were subject to codetermination in 1976. By the early 1980s, codetermination covered only about 480 firms. About 120 firms had reduced their labor force below the 2000 limit, while about 50 firms had changed their corporate charters.

REFERENCES

Coase, R. (1988), *The Firm, the Market, and the Law*, Chicago: University of Chicago Press.
Deepak, Lal (1998), *Unintended Consequences*, Cambridge, MA: MIT Press.
Jensen, M. and W. Meckling (1979), 'Rights and production functions: an application to labor-managed firms and codetermination', *Journal of Business*, **52**(4), 469–506.
Manne, H. (1997), 'The judiciary and free markets', *Harvard Journal of Law and Public Policy*, **21**(1), pp. 11–37.
Posner, R (2003), *Economic Analysis of Law*, Boston and Toronto: Little, Brown.
Williams, W. (1994), 'Liberals care only about results', *Conservative Chronicle*, 9 February.

PART III

Toward a theory of institutional change

10. The method of analysis

Capitalism is the product of Western civilization. Clearly, Western civilization has managed to create an efficiency-friendly economic system capable of producing innovations in both the market for products and the market for institutions. Toward the end of the twentieth century, the acceptance of capitalist institutions such as the freedom of contract and private property rights helped many non-Western countries to raise their standard of living relative to that of their neighbors. Some obvious examples are Slovakia vs Ukraine, South Korea vs North Korea, and Chile vs Cuba.

However, the fact that capitalism has out-produced all other systems that have ever been tried has not deterred its critics. The critics of capitalism have offered a variety of models, each claiming superiority over the private-property, free-market economy. Some of those models got their chance in the real world (e.g., Marxist socialism, National Socialism, Fascism, codetermination, self-management, etc.) and they all failed to duplicate the results of capitalism. Some models are untested inventions. Addressing scholars who market their own ideologies and blackboard fictions as workable economic models that should replace capitalism, Karl Brunner wrote (1970, p. 563): 'The sacrifice of cognition is particularly easy to detect in objections to the market system introduced by discrepancies between one's desires, glorified as social values, and the results of market processes. However, our ability to visualize "better" states more closely reflecting our preferences yields no evidence that this state can be realized.'

Institutions have predictable effects on economic performance, and changes in the economic conditions of life modify and/or change the prevailing institutions. This two-way relationship between the rules of the game and the game itself provides the window of opportunity for the development of a spontaneous theory of institutional change or, to use what I think are more explanatory terms, a theory of efficiency-friendly institutional change within the framework of tradition. The purpose of this chapter is to outline the framework for such an efficiency-friendly theory of institutional change, which is developed further in this third part of the book.

The proposed theory of institutional change has a positive and a normative component. The positive component requires that the process of institutional change be consistent with economic efficiency. Let us recall that economic efficiency is defined as the process through which voluntary interactions are carried out, leading to unknown results. The key term is *voluntary interaction*. The term '*efficiency-friendly* institutional change' means that, with positive transaction costs, economic analysis can do no more than determine whether the incentive effects of new rules are expected to move scarce resources from lower- to higher-valued uses. Thus a formal or informal rule that offers greater incentives for voluntary interactions is judged more efficient than another rule that provides weaker incentives for free exchange.

The normative component of the theory of spontaneous change in this book says that the process of making rules should encourage the *voluntary* choice of capitalism (e.g., China and Chile vs Cuba and Belarus). The fact that capitalism has outperformed all other systems that have actually been tried justifies including the normative component in the theory of institutional change. Once again, the term 'voluntary' is important. To impose capitalism from above does not work because the transaction costs of integrating its institutions into the social system can be very high. Thus, capitalism has to develop voluntarily and from within the community.

THE CHOICE OF ANALYTICAL FRAMEWORK

Since the days of Alfred Marshall, neoclassical economics has been the mainstream method for microeconomic analysis. In the second half of the twentieth century, the Chicago School made great contributions to our understanding of the economic forces at work. It is fair to say that the Chicago School established the efficiency-friendly implications of non-attenuated private property rights, freedom of trade within and between communities, and open entry into competitive product markets.

The basic assumptions of neoclassical economics are, however, ill-suited to the analysis of economic activities across different institutional arrangements. Three critical assumptions of neoclassical economics that keep it from being a useful method for analysis of institutional change are zero transaction costs, stable and exogenously given preferences, and market equilibrium.

The fact is that transaction costs are positive and not invariant with respect to alternative institutions. Individual preferences are continuously created and/or modified through the knowledge-creating process of exchange, which is also not invariant with respect to different institutions. And market equilibriums are statements about the end results that would be attained if people were free to interact and if relative prices captured all the information that utility-seeking individuals need. With positive transaction costs, such statements have little empirical content.

While neoclassical analysis has provided a powerful analytical argument to understand allocative efficiency in a private-property, free-market economy, it lacks explanatory power when comparing the allocation and use of resources across various institutional structures having different transaction costs. Indeed, neoclassical scholars have often arrived at misleading conclusions about the economic performance of countries having different institutional arrangements. Here is what three well-known neoclassical economists said about the Soviet Union a few years before the country disintegrated from within.

Heilbroner and Thurow (1984, p. 629) wrote: 'Can economic command significantly compress and accelerate the growth process? The remarkable performance of the Soviet Union suggests that it can. In 1920, Russia was but a minor figure in the economic councils of the world. Today it is a country whose economic achievements bear comparison with those of the United States.' Paul Samuelson (1980, p. 624) said: 'It is a vulgar mistake to think that most people in Eastern Europe are miserable ... The gap between Western and Eastern living standard may narrow in the future.' And John Kenneth Galbraith on his return from Russia in 1984 claimed that the Soviet economy had made great national progress in recent years (1984, 3 September pp. 54–63).

In the last few decades, a body of literature has grown around the notion that institutions have predictable effects on the economy.[1] By emphasizing the interconnectedness of institutions, incentives, transaction costs and economic behavior, the New Institutional Economics became a fast-growing method for the analysis of economic and social issues. Being a relatively young method of analysis, the New Institutional Economics is still in the process of finding its way into the mainstream.

A number of scholars see the New Institutional Economics as an attempt to enlarge the ability of neoclassical economics to explain a wider range of events. According to Libecap (1998, p. 4), 'The New Institutional Economics retains its general attachment to neoclassical economics with its emphasis on individual maximization and marginal analysis, but with attention to transaction costs, information problems, and bounded rationality.' Some scholars, such as Erik Furubotn and Oliver Williamson, take neoclassical analysis as a point of departure for redirecting economic analysis toward the effects of alternative institutions on economic behavior. Many other scholars consider the New Institutional Economics to be slowly but continuously developing strong ties with the Austrian and Public Choice schools.

An analytical framework that combines the New Institutional Economics, Austrian Economics and Public Choice is used here to develop the theory of efficiency-friendly institutional innovation within the framework of tradition. In this framework, the effects of institutional incentives and the feedback of their consequences replace the maximization paradigm of neoclassical economics. The knowledge created through the process of making choices replaces stable and exogenously given preferences, and the selection process of choosing among institutional alternatives replaces the assumption of a rational agent who is able to identify market equilibrium in each situation at zero transaction costs. Herbert Simon (1978, p.6) said it well: '[New economic theories] are not focused upon, or even much concerned with, how variables are equated at the margin, or how equilibrium is altered by marginal shifts in conditions. Rather they are focused on qualitative and structural questions, typically, on the choice among a small number of discrete institutional alternatives.'

Because of the tenacity of informal rules, the theory of institutional change generally refers, unless otherwise stated, to the causes and consequences of changes in formal rules. Yet informal institutions are not written in stone. The theory must then include the causes and consequences of changes in informal rules as well.

THE MODEL

The proposed theory of efficiency-friendly institutional change is based on the interaction thesis, on two postulates and on three building blocks. Transaction costs and incentives connect the postulates and building blocks to observed results.

A new rule does not operate in a vacuum. Thus analysis of its incentive effects cannot inform us whether the rule is efficiency-friendly. That is so because the observed economic result of the enactment of a formal rule is the joint outcome determined, not only by the incentives it generates, but also by the reaction it gets from other formal and informal rules. For that reason, the central argument of my analysis is that culture (informal rules) and formal rules play an important role in economic development, not in themselves but in interaction with each other. The interaction thesis is explained in Chapter 11.

The postulates are the rule of law and the market for institutions. Discussion of the rule of law is in Part II, but it is worth reemphasizing a few points. The rule of law has three key elements: equality before the law, absence of arbitrary power, and a mechanism for replacing the ruling group. The rule of law is like a container that holds institutions consistent with those elements. It is also the foundation from which capitalism has emerged and upon which it rests. This means that the four basic institutions of capitalism, private property rights, the law of contract, an independent judiciary, and a constitution are essential parts of the rule of law. That is so because the rule of law reduces the transaction costs of identifying and exploiting exchange opportunities, creates incentives to accept risks associated with creating new opportunities for exchange (entrepreneurship) and eliminates the bias against decisions that have long-lived consequences.

Through their effects on human behavior and transaction costs, four basic institutions of capitalism affect economic performance in two different ways. Private property rights and the law of contract create incentives that move re-

sources to their highest-valued uses and, in the process of doing so, they help
to determine who gets what and who does what. The role of the other two institutions is to protect the efficiency-friendly incentives of private property rights
and the law of contract. We have seen in Part II that the rule of law is a useful
yardstick against which we can evaluate the prevailing institutions in any country as well as the efficiency incentives of institutional reforms. We have also
seen, in Chapter 8, that changes in the rule of law are a good predictor of economic performance.

As for the market for institutions, we observe that formal rules keep changing.
Informal rules also change, but more slowly. Thus markets for formal and informal institutions exist. The issue is then not their existence, which is obvious,
but their economic efficiency. An efficiency-friendly market for institutions has
two functions: to create incentives for institutional innovation and to reduce the
transaction costs of adaptive behavior. The former provides individuals with
freedom to seek changes in the rules of the game. The latter assures the community of freedom to accept or reject proposed institutional changes. The
voluntary acceptance of institutional change signals that the community is better
off.

Major determinants of the efficiency of the market for institutions, then, are
the incentives of rule makers, the procedures for making rules, the constraints
under which rule makers operate, competitive product markets with cheap entry
and exit, and non-regulated financial markets. As the incentives and constraints
of common law judges are not the same as those of elected representatives, the
choice of the legal system matters.

We observe that the demand for formal rules and regulations often comes
from organized groups, rent-seeking coalitions, ideological movements and
other organizations that wield or seek political power. It would be naïve and
empirically empty to base analysis on the assumption that it is possible to
eliminate discretionary use of political or economic power in the process of
making new rules. It is, however, possible to develop constraints that would
raise the costs of rule makers' responsiveness to political and economic pressure
groups. Once again, the choice of legal system is important because common
law and civil codes create different sets of constraints.

It is easy to assert that new rules have to be voluntarily accepted by the community. It is more costly to put that requirement into action. Thus it is useful to
look for proxies that justify new formal rules. Competitive product markets are
such a proxy. That is so because competitive product markets separate the rules
enacted in response to the changing requirements of the game from the rules
enacted from above with the intent of changing the game. Suppose a technological innovation passes the market test. Clearly, it has made the community better
off. Otherwise, the innovation would have failed, as many do. However, if the
prevailing rules left some potential opportunities for gains from this innovation

unexploited, it is arguable that, by accepting the innovation in the product market, the community has implicitly agreed to accept a new rule that would reduce the transaction costs of exploiting exchange opportunities from that innovation. Forthcoming chapters offer several examples.

To develop the market for institutions, capitalist countries would have to strengthen, admittedly by *fiat,* the basic institutions of capitalism, while non-capitalist countries would have to enact, also by *fiat*, those same formal rules.

The building bocks of the theory are the carriers of change, formal rules and informal institutions. They are discussed in Chapters 12 to 14.

NOTE

1. The interest in institutions is not new. At the beginning of the last century, T. Veblen, J. Commons and W. Mitchell, among others, developed what became known as the American Institutionalist School. However, this school quickly petered out for failing to develop the theory of the effects of institutions on the economy as well as the evidence for refutable implications of those effects.

REFERENCES

Brunner, K. (1970), 'Knowledge, values, and the choice of economic organization', *Kyklos*, **23**(3), 558–80.
Galbraith, J.K. (1984), 'A visit to Russia', *New Yorker*, **60**, September.
Heilbroner, R. and L. Thurow (1984), *Economic Problem*, New York: Prentice-Hall.
Libecap, G. (1998), 'The New Institutional Economics and economic development', *ICER Working Paper Series*, 15.
Samuelson, P. (1980), *Economics,* New York: McGraw-Hill.
Simon, H. (1978), 'Rationality as a process and as a product of thought', *American Economic Review*, **68**(2), 1–16.

11. The interaction thesis

Institutional change generally refers to the enactment of formal rules. A new formal rule can be out of tune with other formal rules. However, formal rules are a policy variable and the government can take care of old rules that conflict with the new one. The government can also change the new formal rule to accommodate the old ones. On the other hand, the government can do little and perhaps nothing about conflict arising between formal and informal rules because the latter are not a policy variable. Hence the focus of analysis is on the relationship between new formal and prevailing informal rules. The process and implications of changes in informal institutions or culture are discussed in Chapter 14.

A new formal rule creates new choices for human interactions or modifies the old ones. In either case, it changes the opportunity set within which the game is played. The effect of this new rule on economic performance must then depend on how individuals perceive and subjectively evaluate new tradeoffs. It follows that the interaction of a new rule with other rules is critical because some new rules enhance coordination and cooperation with informal institutions, while some do not.

The prevailing culture thus plays a major role in determining the transaction costs of integrating the new rule into the prevailing institutional structure. Transaction costs specific to the reaction of the prevailing culture to the enactment of a new formal rule include the effect of the new rule on the predictability of behavior, the risks associated with non-routine behaviors imposed by the new rule, the estrangement of those who are quicker to accept the new rule from friends and neighbors who are slower in abandoning old rules, sunken investments in the prevailing informal rules, and the resistance of the groups and coalitions that stand to gain from preserving the status quo.

The relationship between new formal rules and the prevailing informal rules, which I call *the interaction thesis*, can be summarized as follows:

> When the members of the community perceive the consequences of a new formal rule to be in conflict with their prevailing culture, the transaction costs of integrating that rule into the institutional framework will be high, consume more resources, and reduce the production of wealth. And when the members of the community perceive the consequences of a new formal rule to be in harmony with their prevailing culture, the transaction costs of integrating that rule into the institutional framework will be low, consume fewer resources, and increase the production of wealth.

The actual economic outcome is the *joint* product of the interaction of a new rule with the prevailing informal rules. It means, and this is an important point, that there is no way to tell how much a new formal rule has contributed to the total result.

Finally, conflict between the prevailing culture and a new formal rule reveals itself in three major ways. The first is when the government decides to repeal a formal rule. A good example is the XVIII amendment to the United States Constitution ratified on 16 January 1919. The amendment prohibited the manufacture, sale and importation of liquors. It turned out to be completely out of tune with the American culture of social drinking. The consequence of this amendment was an increase in illegal production and sale of liquor, which the government could not stop. The issue was, in fact, much more serious than the freedom to drink. The issue was freedom from having the elite decide the terms on which people live and socialize. On 5 December 1933, amendment XXI repealed amendment XVIII. Thus the same activity that would have put an individual in jail before 5 December 1933 instead began to make positive contributions to GDP after that date. In a similar vein, I conjecture that the failure of the bureaucrats in Brussels to get the EU constitution approved was a consequence of conflict between the proposed document and the prevailing informal institutions in a region that has many different cultures.

The second way in which conflict between new formal rules and the prevailing culture is revealed involves the costs of enforcement. A good example is investment the former Soviet Union had to make in its control apparatus – the KGB, regular police, and gulags (forced labour camps) – in order to enforce its formal rules. On a less alarming level, the formal rule that limited the maximum speed on American highways from 75 miles to 55 miles per hour in the 1970s was in conflict with the driving culture of most Americans. The enforcement of this rule being in the province of the states led to different results. Some states (mostly northern) chose to incur high enforcement costs, while other states (mostly southern) were quite lax in enforcing speed limits. Finally, the rule was changed (in some cases on a state-by-state basis) and the conflict with the driving culture of American people was reduced.

Conflict between a new formal rule and informal institutions often compels governments at all levels to enact secondary or follow-up laws and regulations. The stated intent of those laws and regulations is to reduce the conflict arising between new formal institutions and informal rules. However, the consequence of all secondary laws is more dirigisme from above. Eventually, communities end up with government-engineered compromises between new formal rules and informal rules. And the costs of those compromises are borne by all citizens regardless of whether they wanted institutional reforms, opposed them, or did not care one way or the other.

THE VALIDITY OF THE INTERACTION THESIS: THE AMERICAN WEST

The economic development of the American West is a good example of what happens when new formal rules are in tune with the prevailing culture. In a relatively short period of time, the low transaction costs of integrating formal and informal rules converted undeveloped Midwest prairies, uninviting Southwest plains and the less than hospitable Rockies into one of the most affluent parts of the world. It happened because new formal rules subsumed prevailing informal institutions.

Gary Libecap described the development of informal property rights arrangements in the American West and their eventual enactment into formal rules (1996, p. 57) as follows: As 'the mining industry boomed, spurred by huge ore discoveries … pressure on existing legal institutions forced new ownership structure to emerge. This resulted in the observed progression in mineral rights law from general, unwritten rules in the 1850s to highly specified statutes and court verdicts by the end of the century'. Harold Demsetz (1967) demonstrated that the development of private property rights did not require the state. Fred McChesney (1990) provided evidence that the transaction costs resulting from the attenuation of private property rights in land by the United States government explain the plight of American Indians.

Terry Anderson and Peter Hill offer interesting and useful analysis through their story of the economic development of this frontier in a delightful book, *The Not So Wild, Wild West* (2004). People who took it upon themselves (long before the state moved in) to advance the frontier westward were rugged individualists. The risk they accepted was tremendous, but they were driven by desire to seek and accumulate wealth and, in the process of seeking to increase their personal wealth, the settlers gave us powerful evidence that a society of free and self-responsible individuals could create, almost overnight, enormous wealth in a region that had seen no economic development of any consequence for centuries.

The following paragraph (Anderson and Hill, p. 8) captures the essence of what really happened in the American West. Moreover, the explanation is consistent with the interaction thesis that low transaction costs of integrating formal and informal rules encourage economic development. That is so because transaction costs tend to be low whenever formal rules subsume local traditions and customs.

Property rights that evolve from the bottom-up – as opposed to the top down – are much more likely to conserve resources and promote investment. The opposite is also true; when property rights are dictated from central authorities with fewer stakes in the outcome, time and effort are often wasted in the process of creating the property rights, and productive investment suffers. Just as technological change is usually incremental rather than discontinuous, [spontaneous] institutional change evolves slowly, taking into account specific conditions of time and place. Developing countries generally and the former communist countries in particular are finding out just how hard it is to nurture this evolutionary process. We believe that important lessons can be learned from the American West, where institutional evolution trumped institutional revolution.

THE VALIDITY OF THE INTERACTION THESIS: THE TRANSITION IN CENTRAL AND EASTERN EUROPE

The intention of new leaders in the early 1990s was to transform Central and East European (C&EE) countries into free-market, private-property economies. Their choice of capitalism seemed quite rational. After decades of oppressive socialism and economic deprivations, people in C&EE were hoping for more freedom and better economic conditions of life. The road to capitalism was seen as being merely a technical problem. East Europeans were expected to perceive new opportunities quickly, evaluate their consequences, and make the utility-maximizing choices. Privatized assets, regardless of their initial ownership, would then end up in the hands of the highest-valued users. In this scenario, it seemed appropriate to encourage new leaders in Eastern Europe to use the strong hand of the state to build capitalism.

Some scholars disagreed with this approach to the transition process in C&EE. For years, since long before the end of socialism in C&EE, James Buchanan has been highly critical of economic analysis that treats economic issues as technical problems. He wrote (1976, p. 2): 'The principle that exposure to economics should convey is that of the spontaneous coordination, which the market achieves. The central principle of economics is not the maximization of objective functions subject to constraints. Once we become methodologically trapped in the maximization paradigm, economics becomes applied mathematics or engineering.' My early opposition to the imposition of capitalism from above (Pejovich, 1994, p. 524) was also clear: 'The transition process *via* exogenous changes could neither deliver the goods nor endear East Europeans to capitalism … by identifying the results of the transition process with capitalism. East Europeans are voting free-market parties out of power.'

Indeed, the imposition of capitalism by fiat produced a host of unintended political and social consequences, culminating in the rising strength of pro-socialist and pro-collectivist parties. The road to capitalism by fiat turned out to be quite bumpy and uneven throughout the region. The rest of this section demonstrates that the interaction thesis offers a verifiable explanation for the uneven results of institutional restructuring in C&EE (Pejovich, 2006).

The prevailing culture in Central and Eastern Europe has a bias toward collectivism, egalitarianism and shared values, and that bias pre-dates communism.

The community in C&EE tends to be seen as an organic whole in which individuals are expected to subordinate their private ends to the pursuit of common values (whoever defines them). Predictably, the extended family has always played an important role in most C&EE countries.[1] It means that, in the early 1990s, the prevailing culture in C&EE was not in tune with the behavioral incentives of the institutions of capitalism.

However, the prevailing culture in the region is not homogeneous. The culture of collectivism and egalitarianism gets stronger the farther east and southeast one travels. Three empires (Austro-Hungarian, Russian and Ottoman), three religions (Roman Catholic, Orthodox and Islam) and the internal strength of ethnicity and/or nationalism explain cultural differences from one region of C&EE to another.

The prevailing culture in C&EE not being homogeneous, the transaction costs of transition differ from one country to another. And those differences in transaction costs translated, at least during the initial ten years or so, into different transition results. Since the culture of individualism is a Western phenomenon, the interaction thesis suggests that the results of institutional restructuring should correlate to the extent of Western influence in C&EE. To verify this proposition, we can divide C&EE countries into two groups: those that have had more cultural and political interactions with the West, and those that have had less or none. It is reasonable to expect that the prevailing informal rules in those countries have retained memories of the rule of law and individual rights.

The Czech Republic, Croatia, Hungary, Slovakia and Slovenia used to be part of the Austro-Hungarian Empire. Western culture entered Poland via the Catholic Church. In addition to playing a major role in the development of informal rules in that country, the Church also helped the Poles to preserve their customs from Russia (including during the post-Second World War years). For centuries, the Baltic States maintained strong contacts with merchants from Germany, Sweden and Finland. In addition to the cultural consequences of this trade, Christianity arrived in the Baltic states from the West. Estonia and Latvia have become predominantly Lutheran, while Lithuania is Roman Catholic. Through religious and trade contacts, Western culture contributed to customs and traditions in the Baltic States.

Table 11.1 divides C&EE countries into those that had greater and lesser influence from the West. Then the Heritage Index of Economic Freedom is applied to measure the results of institutional restructuring. Since institutional restructuring is a process rather than an event, the table shows the results of transition in two different years, 1996 and 2006.[2] As noted in Chapter 8, until 2007, the Heritage Index scales ran from 1 (the best) to 5 (the worst) and separated all countries into four broad categories of economic freedom: *free* (1–1.99), *mostly free* (2.00–2.99), *mostly unfree* (3.00–3.99) and *repressed* (4.00 or higher).

Table 11.1   Economic freedom in Central and Eastern Europe

Country	Economic freedom	
Greater Western influence	2006	1996
Estonia	1.75	2.44
Lithuania	2.14	3.45
Latvia	2.43	3.19
Czech Republic	2.10	2.28
Slovakia	2.35	3.13
Hungary	2.44	3.03
Slovenia	2.41	3.79
Poland	2.49	3.29
Croatia	2.78	3.58
Average	*2.32*	*3.13*
Lesser Western Influence	2006	1996
Bulgaria	2.88	3.50
Moldova	3.10	3.45
Albania	2.75	3.63
Russia	3.50	3.70
Ukraine	3.24	4.00
Romania	3.19	3.40
Belarus	4.11	3.45
Macedonia	2.80	not rated
Bosnia-Hercegovina	3.01	not rated
Serbia & Montenegro	not rated	not rated
Average	*3.17 (3.25)*	*3.59*

Table 11.1 provides striking evidence in support of the interaction thesis, which says that the conflict between the incentive effects of the formal rules of capitalism and the prevailing culture creates transaction costs specific to the process of transition. Among C&EE countries in 1996, the Heritage Index ranked only Estonia and the Czech Republic as *mostly free* countries. All other countries were ranked as *mostly unfree*. The mean rating of the countries influenced by the West was 3.13, already close to the *mostly free* ranking. The mean rating of countries not influenced by the West for 1996 was 3.59.

In 2006, the Heritage Index ranked Estonia as a free country and all other countries influenced by the West as *mostly free*. Between 1996 and 2006, the mean rating of countries influenced by the West improved from 3.13 (*mostly unfree*) to 2.32 (*mostly free*), or by about 35 percent. During the same period, only two countries from the second group, Bulgaria and Albania, moved from mostly unfree to the mostly free category. And the mean rating of the second group of countries changed from 3.59 (*mostly unfree*) to 3.25 (still *mostly unfree*), or by about 10 percent. Adding Macedonia and Bosnia-Hercegovina, which were not rated in 1996, to the group of countries that had fewer contacts with the West improves the mean rating to 3.17.

Empirical observations are consistent with the interaction thesis. This chapter examines two very different cases of institutional development: the bottom-up institutional development in the American West and the top-down institutional restructuring in Central and Eastern Europe in the 1990s. The former rested on the prevailing customs of the early settlers. Predictably, the bottom-up institutional changes led to the development of capitalism and enormous economic prosperity in a region that was completely undeveloped. On the other hand, the imposition of the institutions of capitalism by *fiat* in Central and Eastern Europe raised the transaction costs of their integration with the prevailing culture of the region and brought back to power the old socialist and pro-collectivist parties.

The interaction thesis underscores the importance of the carriers of change, formal rules and informal rules as the key building blocks of the proposed theory of efficiency-friendly institutional change within the framework of tradition. The following chapters analyze these building blocks and their economic consequences.

NOTES

1. Antonina Zhelyazkova described the tradition-driven extended family in Albania (2003, pp. 140–41): 'Family community [is] composed of three or four generations, with a high level of internal solidarity. Within the [family] there is a strict, clear-cut age hierarchy, where the father's ... word is law ... this is due to the age-old internal ethno-cultural mechanism, which ... contributes to the preservation of their tradition.' Similarly, Silke Stahl argued that informal rules in Russia are not supportive of the capitalist culture that values the nuclear family and behavior based on self-interest, self-responsibility and self-determination. She wrote (1997, p. 279) that 'in Russia institutions found their expression in egalitarianism and collectivism. Egalitarianism is the psychological disposition of a group of people who consider material equality as the essential basis of social interaction. Collectivism refers to a societal organizational pattern, which centers on the group and not the individual as the basic unit in society. In such societies the well-being of the group is much more important than the well-being of the individual ... the single person is subordinated to the commune'. As elaborated in Chapter 14, these two quotations portray possible reactions of the establishment when alternative institutional arrangements threaten the old ways.
2. See 1996 and 2004 Index of Economic Freedom, published jointly by the Heritage Foundation and the *Wall Street Journal*.

REFERENCES

Anderson T. and P. Hill (2004), *The Not So Wild Wild West*, Stanford: Stanford University Press.

Buchanan, J. (1976), 'General implications of subjectivism in economics', paper presented at the conference on *Subjectivism in Economics*, University of Dallas.

Demsetz, H. (1967), 'Toward a theory of property rights', *American Economic Review*, **57**, May, 347–59.

Kane, T., K. Holmes and M.A. O'Grady (eds), Index of Economic Freedom, Washington D.C.: Heritage Foundation and *Wall Street Journal* (annual publication).

Libecap, G. (1996), 'Economic variables and the development of the law: the case of Western mineral rights', in L. Alston, T. Eggertsson and D. North (eds), *Empirical Studies in Institutional Change*, Cambridge: Cambridge University Press, pp. 34–58.

McChesney, F. (1990), 'Government as definer of property rights: Indian lands, ethnic externalities, and bureaucratic budgets', *Journal of Legal Studies*, **19**, June, 297–335.

Pejovich, S. (1994), 'The market for institutions vs capitalism by Fiat: the case of Eastern Europe', *Kyklos*, **47**, 519–29.

Pejovich, S. (2006), 'The uneven results of institutional changes in Central and Eastern Europe: the role of culture', *Social Philosophy and Policy*, **23**, January, 231–54.

Stahl, S. (1997), 'Transition problems in the Russian agriculture sector: an historical–institutional perspective', in A. Amin and Hausner (eds), *Beyond Market and Hierarchy: Interactive Governance and Social Complexity*, Cheltenham, UK and Lyme, USA: Edward Elgar, pp. 261–84.

Zhelyazkova, A. (2003), *Albanian Prospects*, Sofia: International Centre for Minority Studies.

12. The carriers of change: the role of entrepreneurs

The carriers of change are individuals. Individuals conceive ideas, formulate policies, convince others to accept their ideas, and bear the cost of failures. Decisions that in everyday language we attribute to governments, corporations and organizations are in fact decisions made by individuals.

The carriers of change make decisions at both levels of social activity. At the level of the rules, individuals carry out institutional changes. In product markets, individuals run businesses. The voluntary acceptance of institutional changes in the market for institutions, and the profitability of one's business in the market for products, mean that the carriers of change have made the community better off. Otherwise proposed changes at either level of social activity would have been rejected.

To distinguish between the carriers of change in the market for products and in the market for institutions, I refer to them as entrepreneurs and pathfinders, respectively. The focus of this chapter is on the effects that entrepreneurship in product markets has on institutional changes. The carriers of change or entrepreneurs are individuals acting in the market for products. They make investments, decide what to produce and/or sell, market their products, capture the benefits and bear the cost of their decisions.

Some entrepreneurs in product markets are doing more of the same, while others are doing something that has not been done before. The former are routine business activities. The latter we call innovation. A major difference between the two types of entrepreneurship is with respect to risk and expected returns. The risk and expected returns from doing more of the same are predictable. The risk and expected returns of innovation are not.

It is easier to define the analytical difference between these two types of entrepreneurship than to separate them in real life. To open a new pizza place is basically a routine investment, but what if the pizza's crust is, for the first time, to be filled with Chinese spices? I conjecture that the innovative aspect in this case is rather trivial. On the other hand, Gates and Dell are unquestionably innovators. Splitting hairs about the exact separation between the two types of entrepreneurship (or the very existence of the separation) would merely deprive us of some important analytical insights. Regardless of whether an imaginary line can be drawn separating routine activities and innovation, some important differences exist.

ENTREPRENEURSHIP AND INSTITUTIONAL CHANGE

This chapter argues that both types of entrepreneurship in product markets make two important contributions to the efficiency-friendly theory of institutional change within the structure of tradition. They encourage the development of formal institutions consistent with the prevailing culture, and they also tend to bridge the gap between the prevailing institutions in the community and the culture of capitalism.

Entrepreneurship and Changes in Formal Rules

The term 'open market' means the absence of legal barriers for the entry of new firms into the market for goods and services. The term 'low-cost entry', however, refers to the time and resources entrepreneurs have to spend actually to begin operating new firms. It is possible for all sorts of red tape to raise the transaction costs of entry into otherwise open markets. The competitiveness of any market depends on the absence of legal barriers for the entry of new firms into the market and on the transaction costs of starting a business.

The more competitive any market is the more incentives potential entrepreneurs will have to move in and increase the extent of voluntary exchange in that market. More voluntary exchange, in turn, creates more knowledge about the opportunities for gains. And more opportunities for gains mean more incentives for entrepreneurs to move heaven and earth to reduce the transaction costs of exchange.

At some point, the prevailing rules might become obstacles to further expansion of the extent of exchange in competitive markets (in closed markets they depend on the choices made in political markets). When that happens, the transaction costs of exploiting additional gains from trade begin to rise. Incentives to reduce the transaction costs in product markets then spill over into incentives to seek a new rule or rules that are more in tune with the changing requirements of the game. Being the consequence of the voluntary interactions of individuals in product markets, the required adjustment in formal rules is efficiency-friendly.

For example, the demand for more exchange in some very competitive sectors of the United States economy, such as communications and manufacture of durable goods, has led to changes in antitrust laws (Kovacic and Shapiro, 2000). The demand for lower costs of production also in very competitive industries, such as agriculture, restaurants and construction, has created strong demand for changes in the prevailing immigration laws. Finally, the demand for more competitive labor markets is growing in European Union.

The first of two unintended consequences of entrepreneurship is, then, the bottom-up change in formal rules. In a nutshell, the easier the entry into a market, the more competitive that market is, and the greater is the probability that efficiency-friendly formal rules will develop to meet the changing requirements of the game. The critical question for the theory of efficiency-friendly institutional change within the structure of tradition is then how to encourage entrepreneurship in product markets.

Entrepreneurship and Changes in Informal Rules

The essential contribution of entrepreneurs is bridging the gap between the culture of capitalism and the prevailing culture. That is so because the owner-managed enterprise is the breeding ground for a work ethic, a capitalist exchange culture and a way of life that rewards performance, promotes individual liberties and places high value on self-responsibility and self-determination. To accomplish this normative objective, law makers have to keep the transaction costs of entry into business low, avoid piling up business regulations and eliminate the disincentive effects of taxation.

For that reason, the argument that subsidies and/or low interest loans are two methods of enhancing entrepreneurship is bunk. Whatever the façade of words, the allocation of subsidies is a political decision, and in political markets the transaction costs of allocating resources to the highest-valued users are high. The assumptions that the government is capable of identifying the most productive users at the same cost or at an even lower cost than competitive markets can, and that the government would use that information if it were available, have neither analytical nor empirical support.

Subsidies and low interest loans attenuate the exclusivity of private property rights. The exclusivity of ownership means that the owner decides what to do with the assets, captures the benefits of the decision and bears its cost. With subsidies and low-interest loans, successful entrepreneurs capture the benefits from running business firms but the costs of their failures are borne by others. Thus, subsidies and low interest loans do not enhance the culture of individualism. In fact, the effects of subsidies and low-interest loans are just the opposite. They strengthen the culture of dependence on the state.

The second of two unintended consequences of entrepreneurship is, then, the bottom-up change in informal rules. Once again, the more competitive that market is the greater is the probability that the process outlined above is going to take place and bridge the gap between the culture of capitalism and the prevailing culture. And, once again, the critical question for the theory of efficiency-friendly institutional change within the framework of tradition is how to encourage entrepreneurship in the product market. I conjecture that the choice of legal system matters.

Entrepreneurship and the Choice of Legal System

In 2007, the Heritage Foundation and the *Wall Street Journal* added two important categories to the Index of Economic Freedom. *Business Freedom* is a measure of how free entrepreneurs are to start businesses, how easy it is to obtain licenses, and, very importantly, how cheap the exit is. *Labour Freedom* is a measure of the ease of hiring and firing employees. It covers minimum wage laws, wage controls, laws inhibiting layoffs and other legal restrictions in the market for labor. In the same year (as explained in Chapter 8), the Heritage Foundation and the *Wall Street Journal* changed the system of grading from 1 to 5 (one being the best) to 0–100 (100 being the best). The new grading system also changed the categorization of countries in terms of economic freedom. As of 2007, scores of 80–100 define free countries, 70–79.9 are mostly free, 60–69.9 are moderately free, 50–59.9 are mostly unfree, and 0–49.9 are repressed.

Those two new categories of economic freedom are good proxies for entrepreneurial incentives to start new firms. Tables 12.1 and 12.2 extend Tables 8.1 and 8.2. Western (in the cultural rather than geographical sense) capitalist countries are separated into two groups. Recall that the first group consists of countries in which common law is the dominant legal system: the United States, England, Ireland, Australia, Canada and New Zealand. Singapore and Hong Kong are left out because it is not clear whether they are part of Western civili-

Table 12.1   Entrepreneurship in common law and civil law countries, 2007

Legal tradition	Type of capitalism	Business freedom	Labour freedom
Common law	Anglo-American	93.48	83.48
Civil law	Continental	85.60	60.70

Note: The scale is 0 to 100, with 100 representing the greatest economic freedom.

Source: Kane et al. (2007).

Table 12.2   Entrepreneurship in major capitalist countries, 2007

Legal tradition	Type of capitalism	Business freedom	Labour freedom
Common law	Anglo-American	93.30	87.40
Civil law	Continental	87.15	60.25

Source: Kane et al. (2007).

zation. The second group of countries includes all Western countries that use civil law: Portugal, Spain, France, Luxembourg, Germany, Belgium, Holland, Italy, Switzerland, Austria, Sweden and Denmark. Left out are Greece, which was dominated by the Ottoman Empire for centuries; Finland, which has somehow remained between the West and the East; and Norway, which uses both common law and civil law. Since business freedom and labor freedom categories were not available before 2007, Table 12.1 shows only the average scores for 2007.

Table 12.3   Entrepreneurship in Central and Eastern Europe, 2007

Country	Economic freedom	
Greater Western influence	Business freedom	Labour freedom
Estonia	80.00	51.20
Lithuania	86.40	60.10
Latvia	76.80	64.10
Czech Republic	61.20	77.20
Slovakia	71.10	62.50
Hungary	71.20	66.10
Slovenia	74.20	48.70
Poland	65.10	56.20
Croatia	53.80	52.00
Average	*71.09*	*59.79*
Lesser Western influence	Business freedom	Labour freedom
Bulgaria	66.90	71.50
Moldova	70.00	61.20
Albania	56.10	60.60
Russia	66.60	66.20
Ukraine	54.00	51.80
Romania	70.90	61.40
Belarus	54.50	64.70
Macedonia	60.90	58.10
Bosnia-Hercegovina	53.80	57.30
Serbia & Montenegro	not rated	not rated
Average	*61.52*	*61.42*

Note: The scale is 0 to 100, with 100 representing the greatest economic freedom.

Source: Kane et al. (2007).

With respect to business freedom, common law countries and civil law countries are *free*. However, the average score is higher for common law countries. The difference between two legal systems is much greater with respect to labor freedom. Common law countries rank free while civil law countries are only moderately free.

Table 12.2 reduces the comparison between civil law and common law countries to four major capitalist states, representing the Continental and Anglo-American capitalism: France, Germany, England and the United States. The comparison confirms the finding in Table 12.1. Incentives to enter into business are greater in common law than in civil law countries. Especially depressing are the numbers for labor freedom in Continental capitalism.

We should also expect that Central and East European countries that have been more inflenced by the West would encourage entrepreneurship better than those states that had experienced less influence from the West. The results are quite interesting. While business freedom is better protected in countries that had more influence from the West, labor freedom scores in countries having a lesser Western influence are slightly higher (better) than in countries with greater Western influence.

ENTREPRENEURSHIP, THE RULE OF LAW AND THE FLOW OF INNOVATION

Innovation means doing something that has not been done before. It could be the production of a new good, the opening up of a new market, the discovery of a new source of supply, the development of a new method of production, or changes in the rules of the game that reduce transaction costs. Whichever the case, by injecting a novelty into the flow of economic life, innovation offers the community a new choice. The implementation of a novelty requires that resources be withdrawn from other uses. By implication, innovation is a tradeoff between (1) the value of the output that resources used by the innovator were producing before and (2) the use of those resources to make an addition to the community's set of choices. Voluntary acceptance of an innovation means that the community is better off.

Most innovations that affect the economy are technological. Technology, broadly defined, embodies the prevailing knowledge. The growth of knowledge then creates new technological possibilities. The innovator translates new technological possibilities into new choices. Accordingly, the innovator must possess traits such as ingenuity, stubbornness, perseverance and imagination. Potential innovators are virtually impossible to identify ex ante, and innovation is not an activity for which we can plan. We cannot decide to have two innovations per month.

The innovator, then, is a true leader of the system, while the rest of the community gets to judge the innovator's entrepreneurial decisions. An implication is that there is no way to tell whether innovations that are not voluntarily accepted by interacting individuals benefit the community (that is, innovations that are forced upon the community by fiat). The voluntary acceptance of innovation is the best evidence that the community is better off.

As I argued before (Pejovich, 1996), if innovation cannot be planned for and if innovators cannot be identified in advance, the best that economic analysis can do is to identify the factors upon which the flow of innovation depends. The four basic institutions of capitalism embodied in the rule of law are critical factors affecting the flow of innovation. That is so because the basic institutions of capitalism enforce individuals' claims of non-interference against the rest of the world, provide protection against all levels of government, and make these claims enforceable in the courts. Hence, the basic institutions of capitalism in effect protect negative rights,[1] and it is negative rights that give individual members of the community both freedom and incentives to pursue innovating behavior *without* using the strong hand of the state to enforce them upon the community as a whole.

Freedom to innovate

To innovate requires the right to acquire resources, and to acquire resources necessitates private property rights. Thus the larger the number of people who have the right to own assets, the larger is the number of people who are free to innovate. In capitalism, all people are free to own assets. It follows that potential innovators in capitalism do not emerge from a specific social class. They come from all social groups. No one could have predicted that John Dell would do what he did out of his dorm room at the University of Texas.

Compare the freedom to innovate for all to various collectivistic agreements. Where the freedom to acquire resources is subject to numerous constraints the flow of innovation is reduced. That is so because attenuation of private property rights raises the transaction costs of transferring resources to the most productive users. Codetermination laws in Germany weaken the protection of shareholders and discourage the flow of innovations. Licensing requirements in Italy reduce the number of people who can pursue specific activities. Restrictions in labor markets raise the transaction cost of hiring and firing people in France. Regulation, such as by the Food and Drug Administration in the United States, delays and perhaps discourages some innovators. In general, attenuation of private property rights and restrictions on the freedom of exchange reduce the number of people who are free to innovate.

Incentives to Innovate

A successful innovation yields benefits in excess of what the bundle of resources used by the innovator was earning before. However, innovation is not a routine activity, and the level of risk associated with it is therefore not known. The innovator has to choose, in effect, between investing a bundle of resources in a project for which the outcome is unpredictable or using those resources in a routine activity for which the risk is known. This is the cost of innovation. The innovator's decision to accept the cost of innovation must depend on incentives.

Capitalism reduces the cost of innovation because the innovator can appropriate the present value of the expected benefits from a successful innovation either in one lump sum (by selling it to another person) or as a stream of payments. The former allows the innovator to exchange the present value of a risky asset (the price of oil from a new well might fluctuate) for stable and relatively risk-free assets, such as high grade bonds. A private-property, free-market economy also provides incentives to innovate to those who do not own resources. For example, the manager of a privately owned firm benefits from a successful innovation via the market for managers, in which the current profitability of the enterprise affects the manager's earnings through competing offers from other firms.

The gains from a successful innovation are temporary. In a private-property, free-market economy, the gains attract duplications and imitations. This means that the innovator's incentives depend on the expected time it takes to compete his profits away. The purpose of copyrights, patents and the like is to extend this lag in order to encourage the innovator. In fact, if all potential rivals were able to imitate successful innovations quickly, incentives to innovate would be seriously impaired. Transaction costs of imitating successful innovations are, however, positive and high. The gap between the novelty and the routine use of resources, which is the source of the innovator's gain, endures because it takes time, effort and resources for potential rivals to learn, evaluate and implement new technology.

The Power to Innovate

Freedom to acquire and use resources is not the same thing as actually having the power to get them. In the private property economy, capital markets match the quantity of financial assets demanded with the quantity supplied to reflect contractual agreements on various issues, including risks. The ability to acquire an asset in financial markets depends on the voluntary agreement between the borrower and the lender.

Another source of power to innovate is the internal organization of the innovator's firm. Its organizational structure and size could create transaction costs affecting the firm's ability to respond quickly and cheaply to the innovator's project. The larger the firm and the greater the number of people who have to say 'yes' as an innovation unfolds, the more costly it is to carry out the innovation. Pat Haggerty, a founder of Texas Instruments, remarked in a private conversation that the firm's top management spent many months trying to find a way to institutionalize the process of proposing, approving and implementing innovations so that the company could retain its leadership in technology.

Integration of Innovation into the Economy

A novelty does not necessarily make people better off. It has to be voluntarily accepted *and* integrated into the economy. In a private property economy, competitive markets evaluate the novelty. Freedom of exchange reveals the costs and benefits of the novelty as perceived by interacting individuals, and those costs and benefits, via relative prices, tell us whether or not the innovation has enriched the community. Large initial incomes of successful innovators are eventually whittled away through market competition via lower prices paid by consumers and higher incomes of resources used to imitate innovations. This means that a successful innovation creates new wealth which is shared by the innovator, resources used to duplicate innovation, and consumers.

THE CARRIERS OF CHANGE AND ENTREPRENEURSHIP IN THE TRANSITION ECONOMIES

One way to test the argument in this chapter is to observe what happened to entrepreneurship in Central and Eastern Europe after the end of socialism.

The bureaucracy of C&EE has hardly changed since the end of socialism. Scholars who belonged to the Communist Party did an about-face, affiliating themselves with Western universities, the United Nations, the European Union, the World Bank and other Western organizations, and they were quickly acclaimed as internationally recognized transition experts. Thus the carriers of change in C&EE, with a few exceptions like Vaclav Klaus in the Czech Republic, Mart Laar in Estonia and Veselin Vukotich in Montenegro, have been individuals who do not see the state as a predator, which the rule of law must tame, but as the leading force in the organization of economic activity.

This means that the carriers of change in C&EE could not and would not appreciate private property rights, an essential requirement of entrepreneurship, but feel more at home with *dirigisme*. While paying lip service to market reforms, Grzegorz Kolodko (2002, p. 76) wrote: 'If there is a choice between developing these [free-market] institutional arrangements spontaneously (*by chance*) or in a way directed by the government (*by design*), then the latter op-

Toward a theory of institutional change

tion is more suitable in the case of post-socialist countries. Even if a small government is sometimes better than a larger one, often government cannot be downsized without causing economic contraction and deterioration in the standard of living.'

Given such carriers of change, the focus of the process of transition, at least in the 1990s, was on macroeconomic policies, the privatization of state-owned firms and free prices, while the critical issue of bridging the gap between the mere enactment of private property rights, on the one hand, and the credibility and stability of private property rights, on the other, was ignored. Predictably, privatization has done little to move C&EE away from efficiency-unfriendly

Table 12.4   Private property rights and government regulations in Central and Eastern Europe

Country	2005			1996		
	Total	PR	REG	Total	PR	REG
Estonia	1.7	2.0	2.0	2.4	2.0	2.0
Lithuania	2.2	3.0	3.0	3.5	3.0	3.0
Latvia	2.3	3.0	3.0	3.2	3.0	3.0
Czech Rep.	2.4	2.0	3.0	2.3	2.0	1.0
Slovakia	2.4	3.0	3.0	3.2	3.0	3.0
Hungary	2.4	2.0	3.0	3.0	2.0	3.0
Poland	2.5	3.0	3.0	3.2	2.0	3.0
Slovenia	2.5	3.0	2.0	3.7	4.0	3.0
Bulgaria	2.7	4.0	4.0	3.5	3.0	4.0
Albania	2.9	4.0	4.0	3.6	3.0	3.0
Croatia	3.0	4.0	4.0	3.5	3.0	4.0
Moldova	3.1	3.0	4.0	3.5	3.0	3.0
Ukraine	3.5	4.0	4.0	3.7	4.0	4.0
Russia	3.6	4.0	4.0	3.6	3.0	3.0
Romania	3.6	4.0	4.0	3.4	4.0	4.0
Belarus	4.0	4.0	5.0	3.4	3.0	3.0
Averages	2.8	3.3	3.4	3.3	2.9	3.1
	(2.1)	*(1.5)*	*(2.7)*	*(2.3)*	*(1.5)*	*(2.5)*

Note: The scale is 1 to 5, with 1 representing the greatest economic freedom. Total, PR and REG denote the scores for the total, property rights, and government regulation categories, respectively. The figures in parentheses are averages for six Western countries: France, Germany, Italy, Spain, the United Kingdom and the United States.

Source: Miles et al. (2005).

dirigisme. State-owned dinosaurs had out-of-date assets. Their employees were accustomed to a paternalistic environment. Managers were members of the old ruling elite or fellow travelers. Moreover, business managers and the employees of state-owned firms frequently negotiated with the legislators and bureaucrats mutually favorable methods of privatization. Indeed, many C&EE countries have adopted privatization schemes that can easily be characterized as stealing (Milovanovich, 2007).

Table 12.4 provides evidence that the failure to replace the carriers of change in C&EE had consequences for the development of private property rights and freedom from the state. The scores for property rights and government regulation are *below* those of other categories considered in the Index of Economic Freedom. The overall mean score of the top eight countries, which had been open to the West before the imposition of socialism, improved from 3.1 to 2.3 between 1996 and 2005, yet their average scores for property rights remained the same (2.6), and the average score for government regulation worsened from 2.6 to 2.8. The lower eight countries, which had experienced less influence from the West (with one exception, Croatia), show a greater divergence between the overall score, on the one hand, and the average scores for private property rights and government regulations, on the other. Although their overall scores slightly improved, from 3.5 in 1996 to 3.3 in 2005, average scores for private property rights and government regulations worsened from 3.3 to 3.9, and from 3.5 to 4.1, respectively.

In spite of the failure of leaders in C&EE (again with a few notable exceptions) to direct their efforts toward the development of never-privatized, owner-managed firms, the consensus is emerging in C&EE that never-privatized enterprises have been the most important contributing factor to economic performance in the region (Winiecki, 2002; Laki, 2002; Dabrowski, 2002). It is hard not to wonder what a different group of carriers of change might have accomplished in the 1990s.

NOTE

1. On the other hand, positive rights, such as a right to free public education, call for interference by the state.

REFERENCES

Dabrowski, M. (2002), 'Ten years of Polish economic transition', in M. Blejer and M. Skreb (eds), *Transition: The First Decade*, Cambridge, MA: MIT Press.
Kolodko, G. (2002), 'Post-communist transformation and post-Washington consensus: the lessons for policy reforms', in M. Blejer and M. Skreb (eds), *Transition: The First Decade*, Cambridge, MA: MIT Press, pp. 45–83.

Kane, T., K. Holmes and M.A. O'Grady (eds) (2007), Index of Economic Freedom, Washington, D.C.: The Heritage Foundation and the *Wall Street Journal* (annual publication).

Kovacic, W. and Shapiro, C. (2000), 'Antitrust policy: a century of economic and legal thinking', *Journal of Economic Perspectives*, **14**(1), 43–60.

Laki, Mikhail (2002), 'The performance of newly established business firms: the case of Hungary', unpublished manuscript.

Miles, Marc et al. (2005), *2005 Index of Economic Freedom*, Washington, DC: The Heritage Foundation and *Wall Street Journal*.

Milovanovic, M. (2007) 'Property rights, liberty, and corruption in Serbia', *The Independent Review*, **12**(2), 213–34.

Pejovich, S. (1996), 'Property rights and technological innovation', *Social Philosophy and Policy*, **13**, January, 168–80.

Winiecki, Jan (2001), 'The role of the new entrepreneurial private sector in transition and economic performance', The Bank of Finland Institute for Economies in Transition, Discussion paper No. 12, pp. 5–42.

13. Formal institutions

Both formal and informal institutions affect individual behavior. However, unlike informal institutions, formal rules are a policy variable. Formal rules are constitutions, statutes, common laws and other governmental regulations. They usually take a written form and are externally enforced. They define the political system (the hierarchical structure, decision-making powers, the individual's rights); the economic system (property rights, freedom of contract, open entry into all markets); and the protection system (judiciary, police, military).

Formal rules could be institutionalized customs and traditions, whereby they serve the function of making informal rules more uniform, predictable, enforceable and transparent. Formal rules are also enacted in order to accommodate changes in the economic conditions of life, in which case they reduce the transaction costs of playing the game. Finally, formal institutions can also be the outcome of a top-down decision-making process in response to the majority rule, lobbying and the pressure from rent-seeking groups. I conjecture that the first two reasons for making formal rules are consistent with the interaction thesis; that is, they have low transaction costs of integration with the prevailing informal institutions. By implication, those two reasons for enacting formal rules are consistent with institutional change within the structure of tradition.

The issue to discuss is the incentives and constraints under which the carriers of change (i.e. makers of law and regulations) work in common law and civil law countries. The point of departure for analysis is the Public Choice School assumption that the carriers of change pursue self-interest. This means that the incentives and constraints operating on law makers and regulators affect the choice of new rules. According to the interaction thesis (Chapter 11), the choice of new rules informs us, via transaction costs, of their acceptance by the prevailing institutions. Economic analysis must then identify the carriers of change in common law and civil law countries and discuss the incentives and constraints under which they function.

Major sources of formal rules in most common law and civil law countries are judgments entered by judges, laws enacted by legislatures, and regulations issued by the executive branch of government. All common law countries have legislators who enact rules and all civil law countries have judges who rely on the previous decisions of other judges in deciding their own cases. Thus no country is exclusively common law or civil law country. The terms refer to the *prevailing* legal system in a community.

ECONOMIC EFFICIENCY OF JUDGE-MADE FORMAL RULES

The common law is the body of formal rules that has its origin in decisions made by judges. The process of creating formal rules in common law countries subsumes the hand of the past. Henry Manne put it well (1997, p. 21): 'A common law system does seem peculiarly well suited to the need in any legal system to respond appropriately to new circumstances. In its origin … common law was primarily local, tribal, or customary law, and, probably for this reason, common law judges have always had a predilection to subsume local customs into decision rules.' To reemphasize the importance of traditions and customs relative to reason in the common law, let us recall the words of William Blackstone (1765, p. 69, quoted fully in Chapter 4): 'For the sake of attaining uniformity, consistency, and certainty, we must apply those rules [precedents], where they are not plainly unreasonable and inconvenient, to all cases which arise; and we are not at liberty to reject them, and to abandon all analogy to them … because we think that the rules are not as convenient and reasonable as we ourselves could have devised.'

An implication is that the transaction costs are low for monitoring and enforcing precedents arising either from the institutionalization of informal rules or from the adjustments of the rules to changes in the game (already approved in competitive markets, as explained in Chapter 12). Precedents arising from those two methods of making formal rules represent institutional change within the structure of tradition, and this means that precedents are efficiency-friendly.

As an outgrowth of the hand of the past, common law has never emphasized social justice, the common good or other vague terms legislators and bureaucrats use as the façade of words hiding their preference for top-down regulations. The focus of common law has always been on the protection of individual freedom, free exchange and private property rights. And the consistent protection of individual freedom, free exchange and private property rights means that common law has been in tune with the capitalist culture that emphasizes self-interest, self-determination and self-responsibility.[1] Moreover, common law is not amoral. Only informal rules that meet a shared notion of ethics can survive the test of time. Common law precedents have passed the test of time, not because they were reasoned to be socially just or politically correct, but because they subsumed customs and traditions. Hence the moral context of the hand of the past is implicit in common law precedents.

To say that common law is institutionalized tradition and customs requires an explanation. Translating informal rules into formal laws is not analogous to putting a dime in the machine and getting out the written version of informal rules. Different judges have different subjective perceptions of prevailing informal rules. Their understanding of the basic legal principles is not necessarily the same. It is, then, fair to say that, while the process of creating formal rules in common law countries subsumes the hand of the past, it also bears the imprint of actions by common law judges.

Indeed common law judges can rule from the bench. Bruce Benson (2005) said: 'Courts can follow precedent and explicitly state that they are bound to do so ... They can also legislate new law and explicitly acknowledge that they are overturning precedent.' The fact that judges can rule from the bench raises a critical question: does the common law system have a self-correcting bias that would replace less efficient with more efficient precedents from within the system? The answer to this question depends on the efficiency-consequences of the process of selecting precedents, the independence of common law judges, and the incentives and constraints under which they function.

Incentives of Common Law Judges

Common law judges, like all other people, prefer more satisfaction to less satisfaction. An important question is then whether the prevailing incentives structures under which they work have an efficiency bias.

Many scholars argue that inefficient precedents could result in moving cases from common law courts to private arbitrations and out-of-court agreements. This means that common law judges face competition that could erode their power and prestige. Hence they have incentives to seek and maintain efficient precedents. Moreover, going along with precedents creates more time for leisure, which is an important good for most people, including common law judges.

Unlike legislators who deal directly with individuals and groups, judges in higher courts, where most precedents are made, deal primarily with activities. By making it difficult for common law judges to accept monetary and nonmonetary payoffs, the rules under which common law judges operate reduce the influence of rent-seeking groups.

Thus major sources of utility for common law judges are nonmonetary goods, such as power, prestige and leisure, and those sources of utility make judges sensitive to being reversed by higher courts and eager to contribute to new precedents. Posner writes (2003, p.541), 'An odd feature of [the production of precedents] is that the producers are not paid. Neither the judges nor the lawyers in *Hadley* v. *Baxendale* received any royalties or other compensation for a precedent that has guided the decision of thousands of cases ... The costs to judges of professional criticism are modest, but because the rules of judicial tenure and compensation attenuate the usual incentives that operate on people, judges are likely to be influenced by what in most walks of life is a weak force.'

Constraints on Common Law Judges

Legal decisions entered by common law judges, if challenged, have to pass the scrutiny of higher courts. If challenge persists, the Supreme Court has to rule on the constitutionality of lower courts' decisions. An implicit assumption is that cases the Supreme Court does not choose to consider are consistent with the constitution. This does not mean that reviews of lower courts rulings by higher courts (including the Supreme Court) are always in tune with the prevailing informal institutions and the United States Constitution. And it would be equally wrong to gauge the process of creating new rules by reference to either the character of judges or their mistakes (at all levels). Judges are human beings who have their own subjective perceptions of reality.

Yet the system is reasonably self-correcting. Common law judges know that higher courts can reverse their decisions. Appellate court judges in turn know that the Supreme Court can reverse their rulings. And the Supreme Court justices know that there are ways for the US Congress to rein in the courts.[2] In short, common law judges are reasonably constrained to stay with precedents, which in turn increase the predictability of the legal system.

The Independence of Common Law Judges

One important function of the US Constitution is to protect common law judges from being influenced by the preferences of the median voter, changes in the balance of political power, and pressures from rent-seeking groups. Of course, we are all subject to peer pressure, common law judges no less than the rest of us. But their pay, their promotions and tenure are not influenced by the median voter, legislators, bureaucrats, labor unions or business associations. The same principle is operative in other common law countries. In Canada judges are appointed until retirement and pressures on them are usually minimal. Judicial ability has remained the most important factor in most appointments. By protecting judges from outside influences, common law enhances the predictability of legal decisions, encourages institutional innovation within the structure of tradition and, consequently, promotes economic development.

The importance of an independent judiciary as one of the four basic institutions of the rule of law was fully appreciated by Hayek, Leoni and most law and economics scholars. In recent years, a body of literature has shown that judicial independence correlates with good economic performance. Klerman and Mahoney (2004) found that their research lends 'support to the proposition that judicial independence is one of the key features of the design of a high-quality legal system. It is remarkable that incremental changes in the security of judgeships are so persistently associated with abnormal returns in the direction that we would expect if market participants viewed judicial independence as a good thing.'

A number of examples offered in Part II of this book provide evidence that common law judges in the United States enjoy good protection from other branches of government. However, they have been much less protected from the intrusion of legislators and bureaucrats into the market for formal rules. Those intrusions have had efficiency consequences that are addressed later in this chapter.

The Process of Selecting New Rules

A Michigan Supreme Court ruling in 1919 is an important example of the respect that common law has for private property rights: in the *Dodge* v. *Ford Motor Company* case, the Court held that Henry Ford owed a duty to the shareholders of the Ford Motor Company to operate his business for profitable purposes as opposed to charitable purposes. This decision was never reversed or overruled.[3]

However, in the world of positive transaction costs, no system can be perfect in attaining its goals. A major function of the interaction thesis, then, is to inform us whether a new formal rule is efficiency-friendly or not. As indicated earlier, the common law system has a self-correcting bias that tends to replace less efficient with more efficient precedents from within the system. The argument goes like this: the total set of precedents in a community at a point in time consists of the sum total of efficient and inefficient rules. Since the costs imposed by inefficient rules are greater than the costs imposed by efficient rules, a larger proportion of contested rules will be inefficient. If the litigated rules are decided on some basis unrelated to efficiency of outcomes, the common law efficiency will tend to increase over time. George Priest (1977, p. 72) argued that 'efficient rules survive in an evolutionary sense because they are less likely to be re-litigated and thus less likely to be changed … Inefficient rules perish because they are more likely to be reviewed and review implies the chance of change whatever the method of judicial decision … the tendency of the common law over time to favor efficient rules does not depend on the ability of judges to distinguish efficient from inefficient outcomes.' An implication is that the process through which new rules emerge is more important than the quality of judges.

The efficiency of any legal system also depends on its response to technological changes in the economy. Technological changes create new opportunities for exchange. To capture the gains from those opportunities for exchange, individuals have to enter into mutually beneficial contractual agreements, yet technological changes often make prevailing precedents obsolete. And obsolete precedents raise the transaction costs of exploiting new exchange opportunities. Rules developed to deal with collisions between the horse-driven wagons in nineteenth-century Texas could not be readily applied to the consequences of automobile accidents in the twenty-first century. To reduce the transaction costs

of contracting, new precedents are therefore necessary. Recall the simple example of the siren testing in Chapter 2, where technological change created an
issue for Hamilton and Jefferson. To exploit the gains from this issue they had
to ask the court to define the right of ownership in the noise from testing
sirens.

The accumulation of responses to technological changes creates new precedents or formal rules. The process through which new precedents arise is thus
both *incremental* and *selective*. The former means that legal disputes are litigated
repeatedly in lower courts, and potentially checked and re-checked in higher
courts. The latter means that the precedents emerging are also the rules most
efficient in reducing the transaction costs of exploiting new exchange opportunities. In 1947, Judge Learned Hand enriched tort law by decreeing that a
defendant is negligent if and only if the cost of the precaution available to the
defendant was less than the expected probability of damages to the plaintiff.
This ruling from the bench is clearly consistent with efficiency-friendly
incentives.

Two examples should suffice to illustrate this tendency of making efficiency-
friendly formal rules in common law. In the second half of the nineteenth
century, the discovery of mineral deposits in the American West created new
opportunities for profitable exchange. As discussed earlier, the absence of clearly
defined rights in mineral deposits was a major problem in exploiting those opportunities. The absence of transferable property rights raised the transaction
costs of exploiting new opportunities for exchange. In the pursuit of self-interest,
the original group of settlers got together and defined property rights in mineral
deposits. Their agreement was to be applied to all newcomers as well. The
agreement worked because the benefits from the now defined private property
rights turned out to be in excess of the transaction costs of monitoring and enforcing those rights. However, as the number of individuals moving into the
region increased, common law judges began providing enforcement of those
informal agreements and, in doing so, arrested potential increases in the transaction costs of maintaining and protecting private property rights in mineral
deposits. Thus the initial informal agreements on property rights became common law rules. Eventually, those rules were fully accepted by the state of Nevada
legislators.

The law of limited liability is another example. Technological developments
in the second half of the eighteenth and the first half of nineteenth century made
possible the expansion of trade and mass production of consumer goods at declining costs. However, prevailing formal rules created a problem. The
exploitation of new technological advances required large start-up investment
in fixed assets, which the then-prevailing law of unlimited liability made difficult
to finance. With each partner held personally liable for the entire debts of the
firm, it was too difficult for existing partners to accept new ones. Every partner

could ruin others through incompetence or opportunistic behavior. The rule of unlimited liability also raised the cost of absentee ownership. Not to monitor one's partners could prove costly. Clearly, the prevailing institutional framework was out of tune with the changing requirements of the game.

Driven by self-interest, entrepreneurs sought to resolve the problem of pulling together large amounts of capital. Some types of contracts did better than others and were repeated. By the 1850s, this process of trial and error led to the law of limited liability.[4] This law limited each owner's liability to the market value of that individual's investment in the firm. Investors could now choose their risk. They did not have to worry about other partners. Equity investments were divided into small shares, which were traded in financial markets. And the law of limited liability, which emerged spontaneously in response to changing economic conditions of life, made the corporate firm by far the most efficient method for voluntarily raising large amounts of capital.

The incentives and constraints of common law judges, the selective process through which new rules emerge, and the independence of judges from other branches of government are three major factors that create incentives for common law rules to be efficiency-friendly and allow them to serve as an engine of economic development.

Inefficiencies of Common Law

Two major potential sources of economic inefficiency in common law are the intrusion of statutes and government regulations into the legal system, and the so-called 'activist' judges. The intrusion of law and regulations enacted from the top-down affects both private property rights and the freedom of exchange. In common law, private property rights serve the subjective preferences of property owners, which means that owners decide what to do with their assets, capture the benefits and bear the costs. Private property rights in many civil law countries such as Germany, France and Italy serve the rule makers' hazy vision of social justice and social welfare, which means that a portion of the value of a privately owned asset is transferred to non-owners. Rent controls in some parts of the United States, price controls in the transition economies in Eastern Europe and restrictions in the market for labor in the European Union are all examples of legislative and/or regulative interferences with the freedom of individuals to negotiate the terms of contractual agreements freely.

Robert Higgs (1997) presented convincing evidence on how Roosevelt's New Deal contributed significantly to prolonging the Great Depression by denting investors' confidence in the stability of private property rights. He said (p. 587): 'From 1935 through 1940, with Roosevelt and the ardent New Dealers who surrounded him in full cry, private investors dared not risk their funds in the amount typical of the late 1920s. In 1945 and 1946, with Roosevelt dead, the

New Deal in retreat, and most of the wartime controls being removed, investors came out in force.'

We observe a relatively high degree of top-down regulation of economic activities in civil law countries.[5] We also observe the intrusion of statutes and regulations in most common law countries, including the United States. Yet, as discussed in Chapter 8, common law countries have done a better job than civil law countries in protecting the four basic institutions of capitalism. Interestingly, the 2007 Index of Economic Freedom ranks only seven countries as *free* countries and all seven are common law countries (Hong Kong, Singapore, Australia, United States, New Zealand, United Kingdom and Ireland).

Common law judges, as noted, can make decisions that diverge from existing precedent as well as from the prevailing informal institutions. Those decisions have negative effects on the interaction thesis. The high transaction costs of monitoring and enforcing those rules translate into less economic development. Possible reasons for some common law judges choosing to ignore existing precedents in deciding the cases before them are a craving to get their names in law books, a desire to pursue ideological sentiments, or a strong wish to objectivize their subjective feelings of right or wrong.

Rulings by activist judges, then, should be highly suspect. It is important that the conversion of those decisions into new precedents has to go through the usual review steps. Unless activist judges can produce strong and convincing explanations in support of decisions to 'propose' new precedents, higher courts are likely to reverse them. And reversals happen. Here are two examples from the United States.

A former member of the Boy Scouts of America had his membership revoked when the Boy Scouts learned that he is a homosexual. The Boy Scouts argued that his conduct is inconsistent with the values the organization holds dear. The expelled member sued for the violation of his freedom as guaranteed by the Constitution. The Boy Scouts argued that theirs is a private, not-for-profit organization entitled to have its own internal rules of conduct. The lower courts agreed with plaintiff. The Supreme Court sided with the Boy Scouts.[6]

Students in a school district are required to begin every day with the US Pledge of Allegiance, which includes the words 'under God'. A divorced father of a student sued the school for religious indoctrination, which is unconstitutional. The lower court dismissed the suit, but the appellate court agreed that the school was violating the Constitution. The Supreme Court decided for the school on the ground that the child's mother is the legal custodian and that she did not object to her daughter reciting the Pledge of Allegiance.[7]

LAWS ENACTED BY LEGISLATORS

The common law tradition generalizes legal principles from specific decisions (precedents) entered by common law courts. As old precedents are dropped and new ones are added to the legal system, judge-made rules change the legal system from within the structure of tradition. In the Continental tradition, legal principles are written by experts, debated by various groups of citizens and eventually enacted by parliaments. Relative to the common law tradition, where changes in the rules are incremental and tied to informal institutions or caused by changes in the game, the civil law tradition gives the political elite more room for discrete changes in the legal system. An implication is that the close relationship we observe between the prevailing culture and formal rules in common law countries is weaker in civil law countries. In short, common law is a major vehicle for making formal rules from within the structure of tradition, while civil law is a major method for making exogenous changes in formal rules.

Common law judges need a specific case in order to start the process of creating a new rule. The development of a new rule is then incremental and initially limited to the area of that judge's jurisdiction. As decisions in similar cases accumulate, the initial ruling becomes widespread. However, when the French Parliament and the United States Congress make a new law, that law applies to their respective countries.

The incentive structures and constraints of legislators in civil law countries (and common law countries, including the United States) and those of common law judges are not the same. Legislators have more discretionary power and face fewer restrictions in choosing between, on the one hand, formal rules that institutionalize into the legal framework changing requirements of the game and, on the other, formal rules that are enacted with the purpose of changing the game. That is so because, in common law countries, higher courts or repeated litigation can themselves correct inefficient rules (which stand only in the jurisdiction of the court that made the rule).[8] But to correct an inefficient rule in a civil law country requires a legislative decision to change the rule. Such decisions take more time and resources, while in the meantime the inefficient rule applies to the entire country. This is an important distinction because it reemphasizes the link between culture and common law rules, which is less strong in civil law countries.

A new formal rule often signals the intention of law makers to seek a specific outcome. Examples are affirmative action in the United States, the harmonization of laws in the EU, and privatization laws in post-communist Eastern Europe. In terms of our analysis, the efficiency of a new rule depends on the response of the prevailing informal institutions. If the transaction costs of the integration of a new formal rule into the system are significant, policy makers either have to make clarifying rules and regulations, or invest additional resources in enforcing the rule, or both. Thus the number of clarifying laws and regulations and additional expenses in law enforcement are a proxy for the effects of the new rule on transaction costs. And those proxies are costly. Secondary laws and regulations are costly to produce. Moreover, by creating the perception of frequent legal changes the enactment of secondary laws and regulations reduces the predictability of the legal system, which in turn retards economic development. The enforcement of an inefficient rule consumes current wealth.

The economic efficiency of laws and regulations that force the game to adjust to new rules is at best very uncertain. An important consequence of exogenous rules is a contraction in the opportunity sets available to individuals. That is so because rules imposed from the top down interfere with the terms of agreements that are voluntarily arrived at by interacting individuals.[9] Also, social engineers and public decision makers do not and cannot possess reliable information about the individual's responses to exogenous institutional changes. Finally, those who impose exogenous changes and those who implement them are not the same people. Those whose job is to implement new rules have their own incentives and private ends, which are likely to differ from those of their superiors.

Legislators also want to be reelected and, if so, formal rules enacted by legislators depend on the terms of exchange between their personal morals and their potential gains from 'selling' rules to the median voter and various organized pressure groups. This means that the preference of the median voter (or the majority of voters) in their districts is an important constraint on their law-making choices, and the median voter is influenced by current fads and immediate economic gains.

The role of the median voter should not be exaggerated. The median voter cares about some issues but is unconcerned about many others. Hence legislators have more discretion in choosing new rules concerning the issues not central to voters. For example, people in the state of Utah care a lot about the use of federal lands and they care little, if at all, about US foreign policy in the Balkans. Congressional representatives and senators from Utah will vote the preference of the median voter regarding uses of federal land but will vote however they prefer when it comes to relations with the Balkans.

Predictably, the behavior of legislators resembles that of Santa Claus, especially at election time. They go around promising goods in exchange for votes. We have all heard legislators tell us that we need more schools, roads and hospitals. We have never heard them tell us what is to be given up in exchange for those goodies. And when they try to answer that question they demonstrate their ignorance. A few years ago, the City of Dallas decided to subsidize the building of a new sport arena. The funds were to come from additional taxes paid by people staying in Dallas hotels. The argument was that the sport arena is a free good because the costs are going to be borne by 'foreigners'. The people of

Dallas were never told that the real cost of a new sport arena is the value of another bundle of goods that the amount of money raised by taxing 'foreigners' could produce.

Legislators also depend on rent-seeking groups and various ideological organizations for both reelection and financial support. In most EU countries, labor unions have lots of influence over legislators; hence we observe that senior workers are well protected, while young people aiming to enter the labor market are largely unemployed and on welfare. The behavior of labor unions and other rent-seeking groups is both predictable and rational. They do not exist in order to pursue the efficient allocation of resources. They exist to maximize the wealth of their members. For them, the issue of economic efficiency is a nuisance. In comparison with the incentives and constraints of common law judges, the incentives and constraints of legislators do not push them in the direction of making efficiency-friendly laws. A dissipation of resources is then a predictable consequence of exogenous changes in formal rules.

The most serious external constraint on legislators is judicial review. Judicial review means that courts can declare a new law unconstitutional, yet the effectiveness of judicial review is not the same in common law and civil law countries. In Germany, the court might declare a new rule unconstitutional but the rule stands until the final decision is made by the constitutional court, which could be many years later. In the United States, the court might declare a new rule unconstitutional and the rule is *suspended* in that court's jurisdiction until the Supreme Court makes a final ruling, which usually takes five to ten years. In the latter case, judicial review frustrates legislators' incentives to impose rules seeking specific outcomes that are either consistent with their private ends or that represent their tradeoff with various pressure groups.

REGULATIONS ENACTED BY THE EXECUTIVE BRANCH OF GOVERNMENT

The power of decision makers in government correlates to the size of their agency budgets. The size of their budgets depends on how much their agencies have to do. Making, monitoring and enforcing regulations provides things to do. It is then fair to say that decision makers in government have built-in incentives to keep increasing the number of administrative rules or regulations.

Pleasing their superiors is the major internal constraint of decision makers. Since their superiors want more money for their budgets, a way to please them is to propose more regulations. And those incentives do not correlate to making regulations in response to changes in the game. Instead, they correlate to forcing the game to adjust to the rules, and there is more to that. Bureaucrats have incentives to go into the private sector and make lots of money teaching their bosses how to deal with the rules they helped to create. For example, many employees of the Internal Revenue Services get well-paying jobs in major accounting firms.

Judicial review is the major external constraint on the proliferation of regulations. Its effectiveness, however, is limited by the sheer number of regulations and relative scarcity of judges.

CONCLUSION

Common law judges make formal rules. Some are made to adjust the rules to changes in the game; these are spontaneous rules, for which the transaction costs of integrating into the system are low. Common law judges also have the power to contribute to the making of new precedents. Those rules could be in conflict with prevailing informal institutions; that is, they could attenuate the rule of law. However, credible constraints, a competitive market for litigation and the independence of judges from other branches of government exert pressures on common law judges to refrain from making rules that are not in tune with prevailing precedents and/or informal institutions. In consequence, the power of common law judges to engage in discretionary law making, while not eliminated, is constrained. The result is a significant predictability for common law.

This means that formal rules emerging from within the system promote economic development by reducing the transaction costs of exploiting exchange opportunities and developing new ones. Buchanan (1975, pp. 46–7) wrote: 'The object of the never-ending search by loosely coordinated judges acting independently is to find "the law", to locate and redefine the structure of individual rights, not ab initio, but in existing social-institutional arrangements ... Law is a stabilizing influence which provides the necessary framework within which individuals can plan their own affairs.'

Laws made by parliaments in civil law (and common law) countries have fewer efficiency-friendly constraints. The median voter is an important constraint who often provides legislators with incentives to make inefficient rules. Moreover, the preferences of the median voter translate into majority rule that give more power to the ruling party to impose its concept of social justice on the society as a whole. And those discretionary powers have consequences. A good example is President Franklin Delano Roosevelt's New Deal in the 1930s. The failure of the Supreme Court to protect the Constitution and individual rights from Roosevelt's regulatory and redistributive program had both short-run and long-run consequences. In the short run, those rules forced the game to adjust to new rules. In the long run, they gave rise to the culture of dependence in the United States. It was only in the 1980s that the Supreme Court began slowly, albeit unevenly, to reemphasize the original intent of the Founders.

Administrative regulations issued by decision makers in government have hardly any efficiency-friendly constraints. Given the magnitude of regulations it would be difficult to subject all of them to judicial review. It is fair to say that government regulations are the Achilles' heel of the rule of law countries.

While common law emphasizes individualism and private property rights, which translates into an emphasis on the equality of opportunity, civil law stresses social justice and the public interest, which emphasizes desired outcomes. Being closely tied to the way the median voter perceives social justice, the desired outcome is a shifting concept. Thus the advantage of common law over civil law comes from the predictability (i.e., consistency) of formal rules arising from the linkage with the hand of the past. And, as briefly explained in Chapter 2, a major, if not the major, function of formal and informal institutions is the predictability of human behavior.

NOTES

1. Also the United States Constitution does not mention social justice or the common good; instead it emphasizes individual liberty, free trade and private property rights.
2. Meese, Edwin (1997), 'How Congress can rein in the courts', *Hoover Digest*, no. 4.
3. See 204 Mich. 459, 170 N.W. 668. (Mich. 1919).
4. This is not to say that limited liability was a new institutional arrangement. The concept was known in Venice as early as in the mid-thirteenth century. Perhaps the best source on the corporation and the rule of limited liability in our times is F. Easterbrook, and D. Fischel, *The Economic Structure of Corporate Law* (Cambridge: Harvard University Press, 1991), chapters 1–2. For a different analysis of the rule of limited liability, see R. Ekelund and R. Tollison, *Mercantilism as a Rent-Seeking Society* (College Station: Texas A&M University Press, 1981).
5. For instance, labor-market regulation encourages the use of efficiency-unfriendly capital-intensive techniques.
6. *Boy Scouts of America* v. *Dale* (99-699) 530 US 640 (2000).
7. *Elk Grove Unified School District* v. *Newdow* (02-1624) 542 1 (2004).
8. For example, in the state of Vermont, the prevailing culture favors 'restorative' justice. Common law judges are responding to this culture by giving sex-offenders light sentences coupled with mandatory psychiatric observation. In Texas, sex-offenders are put in jails for many years.
9. It is also true that removal of bad laws (which have contracted opportunity sets) such as minimum wage or usury would expand opportunity sets. I owe this point to John Moore.

REFERENCES

Benson, B. (2005), 'Common law versus judge made law', Working Paper, Florida State University.
Blackstone, W. (1765–69), *Commentaries on the Laws of England*, Oxford: Clarendon Press.
Buchanan, J. (1975), *Freedom in Constitutional Contract*, College Station: Texas A&M University Press.
Easterbrook, F. and D. Fischel (1991), *The Economic Structure of Corporate Law*, Cambridge: Cambridge University Press.

Ekelund, R. and R. Tollison (1981), 'Mercantilism as a rent-seeking society', College Station: Texas A&M University Press.

Higgs, R. (1997), 'Regime uncertainty: why the Great Depression lasted so long and why prosperity resumed after the war', *The Independent Review*, **1**(4), 561–90.

Klerman, D. and D. Mahoney (2004), 'The value of judicial independence: evidence from the 18th-century England', *Law and Economic Working Paper Series*, No. 03-12, University of Virginia Law School.

Manne, H. (1997), 'The judiciary and free markets', *Harvard Journal of Law and Public Policy*, **21**(1), 11–37.

Posner, R. (2003), *Economic Analysis of Law*, 6th edn, New York: Aspen.

Priest, G. (1977), 'The common law process and the selection of efficient rules', *Journal of Legal Studies*, **6**(91), 65–82.

14. Informal institutions or cultural traditions: the role of pathfinders

The rule of law serves to tame the predatory instincts of the state and its enactment of top-down formal rules, while informal rules assure the predictability of human behavior under the protective umbrella of the rule of law. The magnitude of transaction costs reveals the relationship between top-down formal rules and informal institutions.

The present discussion is in accord with the scholars who use the terms *culture* and *informal rules* interchangeably. They define culture as the synthesis of a community's traditions, customs, moral values, religious beliefs and all other informal norms of behavior that have passed the test of time and that bind the generations (North, 1990, p. 34; Gellner, 1988, p. 14).[1] That is why informal rules are more durable than formal rules and change slowly. And the enforcement of informal rules is different from that of formal rules. They are enforced from within the community and lead to rejection by neighbors, loss of reputation, and expulsion from the community.

Since the development of new informal rules is a slow and time-consuming process, whenever formal and informal rules are in conflict, an easy way of correcting the problem is for the state to change some formal rules. However, throughout history, governments have tried to force informal rules to adjust to formal laws and regulations. Such attempts have always met with stubborn resistance. In a well-researched book on Russian culture, Orlando Figes (2002) wrote: 'There is a Russian temperament, a set of native customs and beliefs, something visceral, emotional, instinctive, passed on down the generations, which has helped to shape the personality and bind together the community. This elusive temperament has proved more lasting and more meaningful than any Russian state; it gave the people the spirit to survive the darkest moments of their history.'

Evidence supports the importance of informal rules. If economic development is merely a function of formal institutions and growth policies why has it been so difficult for so many countries to develop? How does one explain the fact that in multicultural countries some ethnic or religious groups consistently outperform others? Why it is that the same formal institutions and policies have produced different outcomes in different parts of the world? Why are privatization laws in post-1989 Eastern Europe having different results from one country to another? Japanese culture has survived American commercial influence. The Serbs preserved their customs through five centuries of Turkish formal rules. Many Vietnamese 'boat people' who arrived in the United States in the 1970s have prospered under a set of formal rules they could not possibly have understood upon their arrival. Indeed, the evidence and a growing body of scholarly research show that culture affects economic development.

Informal rules change slowly, but they do change. An important issue for analysis is to establish whether the factors affecting informal rules come from outside or from within the system. The origin of those factors is significant because the factors affecting informal rules exogenously and those affecting informal rules endogenously are subject to different incentives and could, therefore, give informal rules different imprints.

Analysis of changes in informal rules, and the causes and consequences of these changes, then, is a key step in providing the evidence for refutable implications of the interaction thesis. To accomplish that objective, the following two sections address the factors that change the prevailing informal rules from without, and those that change prevailing informal rules from within.

CAN FORMAL RULES CHANGE INFORMAL RULES?

Richard McAdams (1997, p. 349) has argued that new formal rules are capable of changing informal institutions. He provides numerous examples including laws restricting smoking, banning duels and prohibiting racial discrimination. In all those and similar cases, informal rules did change in order to adjust to the incentive effects of new formal rules.

If McAdams's argument were generally true, however, the perspective of Figes on Russian culture quoted earlier in this chapter would be irrelevant, and most dictators, especially those basing their legitimacy on specific ideologies, would have no problem with informal rules in their respective countries. Yet this is not what we observe. In fact, economic history is full of formal rules and ideologies that have failed to change prevailing informal rules. We also observe many cases where new formal rules have strengthened informal rules.[2]

Hence, McAdams's observations do not have general validity. An alternative explanation is that McAdams failed to distinguish between formal rules that support the already emerging changes in informal rules and formal rules that do not. McAdams might have emphasized formal rules that have merely institutionalized the ongoing cultural changes.

Let us look at several examples of formal rules in the USA and post-socialist Eastern Europe that have failed to change the prevailing informal rules.

1. In *Kelo* v. *City of New London* (discussed in some detail in Chapter 6), a divided US Supreme Court (5–4) ruled that government can take possession of privately owned land against the owner's will and transfer it to private developers when the result will promote economic development. By implication, the Supreme Court forced some individuals to enter into involuntary exchange with government.

The involuntary exchange is not consistent with economic efficiency. The fact that some owners contest the 'taking' of their land is the best evidence that the Supreme Court has ignored the critical difference between the market value of a piece of real estate and the subjective value of that property to the owner. The implication is that the forced exchange not only makes former owners worse off but also violates the concept of economic efficiency based on voluntary exchange.

Moreover, the Supreme Court decision is in clear conflict with the prevailing culture in the United States, which values credible and stable private property rights. The best evidence of this conflict is that most states have enacted or are in the process of enacting constitutional amendments or laws that restrict government land acquisition through eminent domain to traditional purposes (e.g., roads, railroads).

2. The US Congress enacted the Sarbanes–Oxley Act in the wake of Enron's bankruptcy.[3] Legislators interpreted the Enron case as a weakness of the system, which is not true. Bankruptcies are the consequence of changes in demand, or bad management or fraud. Whichever is the case, bankruptcies free resources for more efficient uses; that is, subsidizing inefficient firms reduces the production of wealth. Successful entrepreneur T.J. Rodgers (2005, p. 5), the founder, president and CEO of Cypress Semiconductor, Inc., said the following about the Sarbanes–Oxley Act:

> Now that I understand what it truly is, Sarbanes–Oxley is very counterproductive. We have a senator from Maryland [Sarbanes] who probably has never run anything or ever created a job in his entire life, dictating to America's corporations how they ought to behave. ... I was amazed at the trivial nature of things that Sarbanes–Oxley made a big deal out of. We spend over $4 million to prevent $300 000 from being [misreported] due to the arbitrary timing of the pickup at one of our plants ... There are about 17 500 companies in the United States, and after I get done naming the usual suspects [for dubious practices], Tyco, WorldCom, Enron and the rest, I would have trouble even naming 17, which is one-tenth of 1 per cent. ... We've had a lot more crooked presidents than that. We have got congressmen in jail today to a much higher percentage than one-tenth of 1 per cent. ... So the fact is I belong to a cleaner, more ethical class than those who would regulate me from Washington.

3. Affirmative action is an unfortunate consequence of the Civil Rights Act of 1964. The purpose of the Civil Rights Act was to protect African Americans from discrimination. In 1965, President Lyndon Johnson issued Executive Order

11246. This 'clarifying' regulation required that all private firms having contractual business with the federal government must prevent discrimination. Federal contractors interpreted this order to mean that they had to commit themselves to numerical hiring goals, and affirmative action was born.

Eventually, the scope of affirmative action was expanded to many other areas of social and economic life. In the 1980s, affirmative action became an issue in the admission of students into universities. Under pressure (explicit or implicit) to achieve a racial balance, universities had begun accepting less qualified and rejecting more qualified applicants. Many, but not all, black leaders and other supporters of affirmative action justified this clearly inefficient investment in human capital, paid for by taxpayers, by arguing that a century of continuing discrimination against African Americans provides strong moral justification for discrimination in reverse. They could have said the same thing differently: it is fine to get rid of one set of inequities by creating another.

Evidence demonstrates that affirmative action is in conflict not only with economic efficiency but also with the prevailing informal institutions in the United States. For example, referendums in California (1996), Washington state (1998) and Michigan (2006) defeated affirmative action. On 28 June 2007, the Supreme Court ruled (5–4) that it is unconstitutional to use race to determine which school certain students may attend.[4]

4.   Niksicka Pivara (Niksich Brewery) in Montenegro is known for its excellent beer. The firm has taken numerous prizes in tough European competition. While the firm sold beer all over the former Yugoslavia and many European countries, its main profit came from summer sales along the coast of Montenegro.

The end of socialism in the early 1990s led to privatization of many state-owned enterprises, including the Niksich Brewery. A foreign investor bought a 70 percent interest in the brewery. The buyer paid 16 million German marks (this happened before the advent of the euro) in cash and promised to invest another 25 million marks in the firm. The employees and local citizens kept a 30 percent interest in the brewery. In addition, the foreign investor promised that the average real salary paid to the employees would not fall below the average real salary in the brewery at the time it was purchased. The average salary in real terms was 200 German marks per month.

The employees quickly discovered that in a privately owned firm, shirking, tardiness and long coffee breaks were out, while working discipline was in. In May 2002, just as the tourist season was to begin, the employees demanded, through their local union, a big salary increase of 35 percent. At that time, the average wage in the brewery was 100 percent above the average monthly pay in Montenegro. In addition to higher pay, the employees also wanted the firm to provide a number of nonwage benefits, such as a car for the union, placing a representative of the employees on the board of directors, opportunities for employees to travel abroad at company expense, and earmarking a percentage of the firm's revenue to build subsidized apartments for workers. By the fall of 2002, the owners had had enough. They decided to move the brewery out of Montenegro.

The response from the striking employees and local politicians was quick and reflected their 'understanding' of the right of ownership. They said the new owners had not built the factory, and therefore they had no right to close it down.

The interaction thesis explains the story. The culture of Montenegro was out of tune with private property rights. The example is not unique to Montenegro. Similar 'attitudes' toward private property rights have been observed in some other Balkan states, Russia, Ukraine and Belarus.

5. The Romanovs (1613–1917) chose to isolate the middle and lower classes in Russia from the West. The Russian Orthodox Church played a major role in helping to preserve this cultural isolation of Russia (and the countries dominated by Russia, such as Belarus, Moldavia and Ukraine), and the Church did a good job. Informal rules became a powerful fortress, behind the walls of which most people were able to hide and learn to live with Communist institutions without ever accepting them. Hence Russian customs and culture survived more than seven decades of Communist rule.

In the years following the end of socialism, the Russian Church did more than just guard Russian culture. In response to the entry of Protestant churches into Russia, the Russian Church lobbied the state to prohibit or at least restrict other churches from marketing their religious packages. The justification for trying to close entry to other religions was to prevent the 'Westernization' of Russian culture. In a Serbian daily, Irena Ristich argued that Christian Orthodoxy has turned Max Weber upside down. According to Ristich (2006), the Orthodox Church has raised the costs of accepting the institutions of capitalism by arguing that the pursuit of material wealth interferes with the teaching of the church.[5]

To conclude, in the *Kelo* decision, the Sarbanes–Oxley law, and affirmative action, rule makers have substituted their concepts of social justice and common good for the protection of individual freedom and private property rights. Being contrary to the prevailing culture in the USA, those formal rules have elicited strong resistance. The examples from Eastern Europe show just how far those countries have to go if they are to replace collectivism with individualism, and replace the culture of dependence on the state with the culture of capitalism.

CHANGES IN INFORMAL RULES FROM WITHIN THE SYSTEM

Analysis of cultural changes from within the system rests critically on the concept I call *the margin of acceptable behavior.* The margin of acceptable behavior is the line that separates intramarginal from submarginal behaviors. I submit that the margin of acceptable behavior is the most useful approach for analysis of how and why informal rules change.

Every culture (and every subculture within cultures) has its own margin of acceptable behavior. However, informal rules, durable as they are, are not written in stone. Hence the margin of acceptable behavior is not written in stone either. A change in the margin of acceptable behavior means the addition of a previously submarginal norm to the set of acceptable rules.[6]

To change the margin of acceptable behavior requires an individual willing and able to take the risk of overcoming the objective and subjective costs of carrying out a submarginal activity. Human history is full of successful and unsuccessful attempts by individuals to change the margin of acceptable behavior. Successful cultural changes at the margin range from the social acceptance of interracial marriages or allowing young people to choose their own partners in marriage to truly major shifts like the birth of Christianity. However, the basic mechanism of change is essentially much the same.

Suppose that a new idea or opportunity for human interactions hits a community from without or is discovered within it. In either case, the agent of change – who can be termed the *pathfinder* (so as not to confuse this innovator with the entrepreneur in the market for products) – perceives prospects for personal gain from exploiting those new opportunities. If the new opportunities for human interactions require a submarginal behavior, a conflict arises between the community at large and the pathfinder trying to exploit new opportunities.

Given potential gains from exploiting a new opportunity, some individuals might choose to pursue actions that are below the margin of acceptable behavior. Those who choose to engage in such behavior would attract strong opposition. Most important, they have to bear the costs of swimming upstream. In addition to financial losses, those costs could range from losing friends to losing jobs and alienation from the community.

If the pursuit of a submarginal activity turns out to provide the pathfinder with a differential return, the success creates incentives for others to engage in the same activity. And if the returns from that activity continue to be sustainable (in terms of costs and benefits borne by the actors themselves), we should expect to observe an ever-increasing number of individuals joining in. Eventually, spontaneous pressures will arise from within the system to incorporate the novelty into informal rules. If and when that happens, the margin of acceptable behavior has changed.

Thus pathfinders change informal rules from within the system and, for the process to take place as outlined, it is essential for the four institutions of capitalism embodied in the rule of law to be enforced and not to interfere with interactions within the prevailing informal rules (i.e., not to affect the costs and benefits of new activities). The non-interference of formal rules with the process of changing informal institutions is important because changes in the margin of acceptable behavior should emerge from voluntary interactions within the community. Then and only then will the acceptance of a previously submarginal rule be efficiency-friendly. Let us look at an example from the United States.

In the American tradition, men specialized in earning incomes, while women specialized in homemaking and raising children. Single women were socially marginalized. Unwed mothers were not socially acceptable. Wives went to work in order to pay some specific expenses, such as a mortgage, or between pregnancies, or after kids went to college. Those informal rules had their economic consequences. Relative to that of men, the leaving rate of women was high. Thus the costs of hiring women and their on-the-job training were, in general, high relative to the costs of hiring men. Predictably, women earned less than men in the same or similar jobs. The difference in pay was the market-adjusted compensation for higher costs of hiring women and their on-the-job training. The real cost was borne by career-oriented women because the transaction costs (as discussed in Chapter 2) of identifying them are high.

Changes in the opportunity costs of being a homemaker in the United States can be traced to the 1960s. Critical factors affecting the opportunity costs of staying at home were the growth of wages relative to the value of housekeeping, and an enormous increase in the range of durable consumer goods available in product markets. And those factors led to a significant increase in women's participation in the labor force.

In a private-property, free-market economy, profit-seeking employers were expected to bid for the services of women doing the same work as men and, in the process, drive their wages up. However, it didn't happen; at least, not right away. The competitive market for labor kept women's wages below those of men, and that outcome was in fact fully predictable. Informal institutions were not in tune with new opportunities for exchange; the game had changed, but the rules of the game didn't. Hence the labor market continued to treat women as a high-cost resource relative to men.

Pressure on legislators to equalize money incomes of men and women came from various feminist groups, which identified the income differences with discrimination based on sex. Such pressures raised the transaction costs of monitoring and enforcing employment contracts but could not address the real issue. The competitive market for labor was not discriminating against women; it was responding to the incentives and constraints of the traditional family. For that reason, the enactment of formal rules mandating something like 'equal pay for equal work' would only raise the transaction costs of integrating these rules with the prevailing informal rules.

The real issue for women was to change the prevailing culture, so that the competitive market for labor would have no reason to differentiate between men and women. This meant that, to capture the maximum potential gains from their joining the labor force, women had to engage in behaviors that would lead to changes in the margin of acceptable behavior. And they did. In fact, the true pathfinders were career women who worked as hard as men for less money and, in the process, bore the costs of disregarding numerous social and economic obstacles. Other women followed in their footsteps.

Eventually, pathfinders brought about changes in a number of rules that stood in the way of their competing as equal with men. In today's United States the margin of acceptable behavior includes acceptance of contraception, single motherhood and live-in arrangements. We also observe that some rules, such as abortion laws and simplified divorce proceedings, have also been institutionalized into formal rules.[7] Those changes in the rules of the game, totally unthinkable just a few decades ago, have slowly but surely adjusted the rules of the game to changing requirements of the game and have provided women with opportunities to compete in the labor market as equal to men.

CONCLUSION

The analysis in this chapter suggests that economic forces at work in the community can and do initiate changes in the game. If and when those changes create opportunities for personal gain (pecuniary as well as nonpecuniary, such as choosing one's partner in marriage), the carriers of change emerge from within the community and seek to exploit them. Depending on the costs and benefits they have to bear, pathfinders may end up changing the prevailing informal rules via lowering the margin of acceptable behavior. Being the result of voluntary interaction within the community, a change in informal rules is efficiency-friendly.

The carriers of change can also fail if and when the costs of lowering the margin of acceptable behavior exceed the benefits. For example, the Amish people in the United States have gauged those costs as too high and have chosen to maintain their prevailing traditional culture. They prefer their established ways even when these entail a more modest standard of living. Most other people are more willing to undertake cultural shifts in order to reach for the benefits of economic progress and modern life, though some kind of wrenching may nevertheless be involved. An implication is that lowering the transaction costs of carrying out submarginal activities increases the rate of change in informal rules.

The rule of law does precisely that. The rule of law creates a protective umbrella under which the pathfinder has only to deal with the (endogenous) transaction costs arising from the community's resistance to changes in the margin of acceptable behavior. That is so because the noninterference of formal rules with pathfinder's activities eliminates exogenous transaction costs of changing informal rules.

NOTES

1. Gellner defined culture as 'a distinct way of doing things which characterizes a given community'.
2. In a remarkable book, *The Years Grasshoppers Ate*, Bora Pekic, a leading Serbian writer and a member of the Serbian Academy of Arts and Sciences, provides some striking insights based on eight years in Tito's jails. Unfortunately, the book is not available in English.
3. The issue yet to be tested is whether the Sarbanes–Oxley Act violated the tenth amendment to the Constitution, for the Constitution did leave the governance of business firms to the States.
4. *Parents Involved in Community Schools* v. *Seattle School District No 1*, Decision No. 5–908, 28 June 2007
5. To say that Eastern Orthodox churches, including the Russian Church, have historically shunned the culture of individualism is merely a factual observation, which does not imply a judgment about the worthiness of their religious beliefs and dogmas.
6. I use the terms *lowering* and *changing* the margin of acceptable behavior interchangeably.
7. Although pressure for abortion came from within the culture and it has now been institutionalized via formal rules, it continues to provoke fierce resistance, indicating that, even when changes are coming from within the system, they can produce continuing resistance.

REFERENCES

Figes, O. (2002), *Natasha's Dance: A Cultural History of Russia*, New York: Picador.

Gellner, E. (1988), *Plough, Book and Sword*, London: Collins Harvill.

McAdams, R. (1997), 'The origin, development, and regulation of norms', *Michigan Law Review*, **96**(2), 338–433.

North, D. (1990), *Institutions, Institutional Change and Economic Performance*, Cambridge: Cambridge University Press.

Pekich, B. (1990), 'Godine Koje si Pojeli Skakavci', Belgrade: Jedinstvo.

Ristich, I. (2006), 'Christian orthodoxy and capitalism', *Politika*, 10 December.

Rodgers, T. (2005), 'Sarbanes–Oxley is worse than flawed; it is pointless', *Directorship*, www.directorship.com, July–August.

15. Efficiency-friendly institutional change within the structure of tradition

This book is intended to examine how the process of institutional change has a bearing on differences observed in economic progress. The term *efficiency-friendly* recognizes that, in a world of uncertainty and incomplete information, we can never be sure whether an outcome of human interactions is efficient. The best we can do is to determine whether the prevailing system of incentives and constraints encourages human interactions that are consistent with economic efficiency. The term 'tradition' means a set of rules that have been at the heart of the institutional landscape in the West since the birth of capitalism and that are respectful of the wisdom of the past.

Analysis throughout the book is consistent and is supported by evidence: institutions, formal and informal, create their own behavioral incentives. Different incentives have different effects on the transaction costs. Different transaction costs have different effects on the extent of exchange, the supply of entrepreneurship, and the integration of new rules into the prevailing system. And the extent of exchange, the supply of entrepreneurship and the integration of new rules into the system are major determinants of economic performance.

THE THEORY

This theory of efficiency-friendly institutional change posits that the four basic institutions of capitalism – (the law of contract, private property rights, a constitution and an independent judiciary, together constituting the rule of law) – promote economic progress because of their incentive effects (reducing the transaction costs of exchange opportunities; encouraging acceptance of risk; eliminating bias against long-lived consequences; and enhancing adoptive behavior) and the efficiency of that economic progress depends on the interaction between formal and informal institutions.

The key components of the proposed theory are the rule of law, the market for institutions, the interaction thesis, the carriers of change, and formal rules and informal institutions. Transaction costs and incentives explain and predict the effects of these key elements of the proposed theory on observed results. Let us summarize the findings about the contribution of each of those components to the proposed theory.

The Rule of Law

The rule of law is the foundation from which capitalism has emerged and upon which it rests. The four basic institutions of capitalism embodied in the rule of law are the law of contract, private property rights, a constitution and an independent judiciary. Private property rights and the law of contract generate efficiency-friendly incentives that move resources to their highest-valued uses. An independent judiciary and a constitution protect those incentives from decision makers in government, rent-seeking coalitions, and majority rule. The incentive effects of these four institutions (1) reduce the transaction costs of identifying and exploiting all exchange opportunities (allocative efficiency); (2) encourage the acceptance of risks associated with creating new opportunities for exchange (entrepreneurship); (3) eliminate the bias against decisions that have long-lived consequences; and (4) enhance adoptive behavior.

Private property rights, the law of contract, an independent judiciary and the constitution have been attenuated to different degrees in Anglo-American and Continental capitalism as well as between individual countries within both systems. However, all four institutions satisfy one critical requirement of the proposed theory: they have been components of the institutional landscape in the West since the birth of capitalism. And it is less costly to enforce or reinforce existing institutions that have passed the test of time than to search for, develop and enact never-tested rules.

The Market for Institutions

The market for institutions exists, and the best evidence is that formal rules keep changing, while informal rules also change, but more slowly. The issue, then, is not the existence of competitive markets for institutions but their economic efficiency. A set of institutions that offers greater incentives for new rules to emerge and reduces the transaction costs of their voluntary acceptance is more efficient than another set of institutions that provides weaker incentives. And the low transaction costs of the voluntary acceptance of institutional change signals that the community is better off.

Under the umbrella of the rule of law, the efficiency of the market for institutions depends on the incentives of rule makers, the procedures for making rules and the constraints under which rule makers operate. Analysis must then address the differences between common law and civil law systems and their effects on the efficiency of the market for institutions.

Common law in Anglo-American capitalism generalizes the right and liberty of individuals from specific decisions (precedents) entered by common law courts. As old precedents are dropped, new ones are added and they work themselves throughout the system. This means that the legal system changes *incrementally*. Civil law in Continental capitalism deduces the right and liberty of individuals from the constitution and formal rules enacted by parliaments. Those rules apply immediately to the entire country. One can argue that, compared to civil law, common law is more in tune with the accumulated wisdom of the past, is less influenced by the preference of the median voter and the will of the majority of voters, and is, thus, more protective of private property rights and freedom of exchange. By implication, institutional changes in common law countries are likely to be efficiency-friendly. Evidence in Chapter 8 supports this conclusion.

The Carriers of Change: the Role of Entrepreneurs

Some entrepreneurs in product markets are doing more of the same, while others are doing something that has not been done before. The former are routine business activities. The latter are innovations. Both types of entrepreneurship make two important contributions to efficiency-friendly institutional changes.

First, the more competitive any market is, the more entrepreneurs will operate in that market and the extent of exchange will be maximized via lower prices paid by consumers. However, at some point, the prevailing formal rules might impede further expansion of the extent of exchange in competitive markets. When that happens, the transaction costs of exploiting additional gains from trade begin to rise. Incentives to reduce the transaction costs in product markets then spill over into incentives to seek a new rule or rules that support potentially available exchange opportunities. Hence those adjustments in formal rules are efficiency-friendly.

Second, the owner-managed enterprise is the breeding ground for a work ethic, a capitalist exchange culture and a way of life that rewards performance, promotes individual liberties and places high value on self-responsibility and self-determination. Thus entrepreneurs help to narrow the gap between the culture of capitalism and prevailing cultures in their respective communities.

The Interaction Thesis

The process of institutional restructuring is about the enactment of new formal rules (informal rules are not a policy variable). A new formal rule changes the opportunity set within which the game is played. The effect of this new rule on economic performance must then depend on how individuals perceive and subjectively evaluate new tradeoffs. And how individuals perceive new opportunities depends on the prevailing culture in the community. The prevailing culture thus plays a major role in determining the costs of integrating the new rule into the prevailing institutional structure. This means that the effect of a new formal rule is a joint product reflecting interaction of that rule with the prevailing informal institutions.

The effect of the relationship between a new formal rule and the prevailing informal rules on transaction costs, which I call the interaction thesis, answers the question: is the new formal rule efficiency-friendly?

Formal Rules

The primary carriers of change in common law and civil law countries are judges and legislators, respectively. However, no country is exclusively a common law or civil law country. The terms refer to the prevailing legal system in a community. An important issue is how and why the incentives and constraints of the carriers of change in civil law and common law systems affect the selection of formal rules.

Formal rules could be institutionalized customs and traditions. Formal rules are also enacted in order to accommodate changes in the economic conditions of life. Finally, formal institutions can be the outcome of a top-down decision-making process. The first two reasons for making formal rules adjust the rules to the requirements of the game. Thus they are efficiency-friendly. Formal rules imposed from above force the game to adjust to new rules. The efficiency of those rules is likely to be accidental or incidental – at best uncertain.

Analysis suggests that the incentives of common law judges, the constraints under which they work and the process of selecting new rules in common law countries are more in tune with the first two reasons for making formal rules than are the incentives of legislators, the constraints under which they work and the process of selecting new rules in civil law countries. Evidence in Chapter 8 supports this analysis.

Informal Rules

Informal rules assure the predictability of human behavior under the protective umbrella of the rule of law. Evidence supports the importance of informal rules or culture. If economic development were merely a function of formal institutions and growth policies, why has it been so difficult for so many countries to develop? However, informal rules differ from one country to another, and people's reactions to the same set of formal rules and policies lead to different and unintended results. This is the way in which culture enters into the process of institutional change.

Chapter 14 defines changes in informal rules or culture as changes in the margin of acceptable behavior. This concept, easily grasped by economists, is useful for analysis of the process of changes in informal rules.

Changes in culture are efficiency-friendly because the carriers of change (pathfinders) bear the cost of their attempts to change the margin of acceptable behavior (i.e., to introduce a new informal rule) and capture the benefits. Hence, if and when a change in the margin of acceptable behavior occurs, the message is that the benefits to the pathfinders were greater than the costs they had to bear (which are the costs of the community's resistance). Changes in informal rules are voluntary and therefore efficiency-friendly.

CAN WE SAY WE HAVE A THEORY OF EFFICIENCY-FRIENDLY INSTITUTIONAL CHANGE WITHIN THE STRUCTURE OF TRADITION?

The answer is a qualified 'yes', based on the fact that the rule of law has been part of the institutional landscape of the West since the birth of classical liberalism and methodological individualism. The theory proposed in this book offers an explanation of why and how capitalism, which rests on the rule of law, has been able to develop new institutions and discard the old ones in response to the requirements of economic development. Most important, the theory treats culture as a critical factor in the process of efficiency-friendly institutional changes.

The transaction costs of institutional changes imposed from the top down are significant. By implication, high transaction costs make the top-down imposition of capitalism in non-capitalist countries difficult as well as inconsistent with the freedom to choose. An alternative approach is to let the community choose to move in the direction of capitalism via voluntary interactions among individuals pursuing their private ends. Toward that end, the involvement of the state should be limited to the enactment, admittedly from above, of the rule of law. The incentive effects of the basic institutions, which the rule of law embodies, would reduce the costs of freely-choosing individuals to determine the direction of institutional changes. Does it mean that they will choose capitalism? I think not. The freedom of choice does not guarantee that individuals will choose capitalism. I conjecture, however, that, in an environment that guarantees the freedom of choice and private property rights, capitalism will win in competition with other types of institutional arrangements.

The term *qualified* applies for two reasons. First, the transaction costs of reversing the attenuation of the rule of law and the intrusion of inefficient rules into capitalism might be substantial, but are arguably less costly, especially in common law, than seeking and trying untested institutions. Moreover, the four basic institutions of capitalism that the rule of law embodies are the best yardstick we have for objective, analytical as well as empirical evaluation of the efficiency consequences of institutional changes.

Second, while a growing body of evidence shows that culture plays a major role in the process of efficiency-friendly institutional changes, only more research can inform us whether the interaction thesis provides a good road map for the theory of efficiency-friendly institutional change within the structure of tradition.

Index